HAPPY
IS THE NEW
HEALTHY

HAPPY
IS THE NEW
HEALTHY

Joan Neehall

with Laura Morton

Forefront
BOOKS

Disclaimer

All names and identifying characteristics have been changed, as have other case details.

Design by Meghan Day Healey of Story Horse, LLC

Library of Congress Cataloging-in-Publication Data is available upon request

Print ISBN: 978-1-948677-70-7

E-book ISBN: 978-1-948677-71-4

10 9 8 7 6 5 4 3 2 1

Dedicated to
my mother

contents

acknowledgments

Most of this book was inspired by thirty-five-plus years of clinical practice.

I'm grateful to my family; to Laura Morton, my coauthor, for her enthusiasm and generosity; to my editor, Hope Innelli; to my copyeditor, Benjamin Holmes; to Adam Mitchell, for his research and contributions; to Meghan Day Healey, for her artistic contributions; and to Linda Loeffler and Kyle Lee for their social media expertise.

Thanks to my colleagues, in particular Jeffrey K. Zeig.

To everyone, especially my patients, I send my heartfelt gratitude.

My mother deserves special thanks for being my major inspiration.

chapter one

. . . .

CHASING HAPPINESS

Happiness is like a butterfly: the more you chase it,
the more it will elude you, but if you turn your attention to
other things, it will come and sit softly on your shoulder.
—AUTHOR UNKNOWN

Few desires in life seem more natural and predominant than that for happiness. In fact, pursuing this desire is one of our most fundamental human instincts. If your basic needs are met and you aren't struggling to survive, there's a good chance you'll be searching for more happiness. Though we all have slightly different views about it, most of us have an idea of what should, can, and will make us happy. Typically, this ideal state includes being in a good mood, achieving a certain level of satisfaction with life, feeling enjoyment, and experiencing positive emotions. Among other benefits, these feelings can motivate us to connect with others, overcome obstacles, and pursue our goals, as well as protect us from some of the harmful effects of stress. Most people make decisions based on whether they think certain actions will make them happy or not. There's an imaginary barometer in their mind keeping score. Although happiness should refer to a state of well-being and contentment, we often confuse it with the here-and-now emotions of pleasure and joy.

When you stop and think about it, chasing happiness often leads you somewhere else—usually to a place that doesn't fill the happiness bucket. I believe happiness is something that shouldn't be hunted down; rather, it should be a state of being, and something we come by naturally, just like breathing. Happiness can become a habit, and a healthy one at that. But it will take some work to get there.

Influential Daoist philosopher Zhuang Zhou (commonly known as Zhuangzi) once wrote, "Happiness is the absence of the striving for happiness."

Exactly!

It's like dating: when you spend a lot of time thinking about it, you usually end up sitting at home all alone. But when you give in to the process and allow it to unfold organically, Mr. or Ms. Right comes along.

Back in the fourth century BC, Zhuangzi talked about the fundamental need people have for happiness, be it in the acquisition of wealth or the search for meaning in life. He discussed it as a purpose and not as a tangible thing to be achieved or obtained. However, I think the latter is often how we treat it today as we hold on to the belief that happiness is out there somewhere, waiting to be captured.

The reality is that the quest for new levels of happiness is never-ending. That doesn't mean you will never truly be happy;

instead, it means that you won't find happiness outside of your-self. It doesn't come from things or even other people. It comes from *within*. It's accessible to each and every one of us, yet most of the time, we walk the wrong path in an unending search for the pot of gold we think awaits us. We've been given bad infor-mation, a lousy map, and faulty directions.

And so people regularly talk about happiness—where to look for it, how to achieve it. They routinely seek specific pathways to becoming the "best version" of themselves. It's a predominant way of thinking that never seems to go away. No wonder we purchase billions of dollars' worth of self-help mate-rials each year! Aside from this book, wasted money. It seems that, even with all of these opportunities to increase our levels of happiness, we've become overwhelmed and unhappy. All the self-help we seek ends up, well, not *self-helping*. We've made ourselves unhappy by worrying about being happy.

Just as we try to avoid physical pain by seeking out physical pleasure, we hope to prevent emotional distress by achieving emotional comfort. The challenge, however, is that our emo-tions are layered and complex, and so they can be hard to truly discern. While we receive direct feedback in our search for physical pleasure, there is often a wall of beliefs, fears, and assumptions that impedes our attempts to get to positive emo-tions.

To ascertain whether we're happy or not, we tend to com-pare past happiness with our current situation—and this is where problems begin to surface. In making this comparison, we place the emphasis on *assessing* instead of *experiencing*. We agonize over this, wondering, "Am I happy enough? Are the people around me happier than I am? How can I be happier?"

How often do you find yourself asking those questions?

What if those are the very thoughts that are holding you back?

Psychologist June Gruber, who has published more than fifty studies on emotional diversity, suggests that striving for too much happiness too often can be a severe problem. She says that when we focus intently on finding happiness, we tend to fall short of the high expectations we set for ourselves. Dr. Gruber's research has also revealed that those who aim for and value happiness the most are *less* able to experience it.[1] Additionally, these people are more likely to endure long-term anxiety, depression, and loneliness. So, when we try to *make* ourselves happy, it's not genuine; rather, it's manufactured happiness, which never lasts. As with many things, when we try too hard, we only end up losing our perspective.

Of course, as we get older, life gets complicated, as do our emotions. When we're unable to cope with situations, we often fall into the habit of tying happiness to external sources or material possessions. We do this because we can't seem to get back to the idea of joy that we established in our minds long ago. Early in life, simple things—such as having a laugh over something silly or playing in the yard with a few friends— seemed to be more than enough to make us happy. When did that change?

When I was a little girl, I used to blow bubbles and then chase them. Every time I caught one or thought I was going to catch one, it burst. I kept at it for quite a while, imagining how magical it would be to hold one in my hand, until I eventually realized that the beauty of this activity was in looking at the bubbles as I blew them and not in the counterproductive act of trying to catch them. I would often do this in the park, and I recall hearing people around me laugh. I didn't know what was so funny at the time. In my naiveté, I assumed they were laughing because the bubbles kept popping or getting away from me. I also thought that maybe the people around me had tried this game and couldn't catch the bubbles, either.

What happened as I grew up? Where did the simplicity of living a happy life go?

Time and experience create specific criteria for what we have to do in order to feel happy, and our belief system sets a course to get there. The upside of this type of thinking is that, when we're feeling down, it fills an immediate need: by envisioning all of the things we wish we had, we're able to improve our mood and adopt a positive mindset about our future, at least temporarily. For example:

"I'll be happy when I meet the right person."

"I'll be happy when I can buy a new car."

"I'll be happy when I lose fifteen pounds."

Who hasn't made those kinds of statements? I know I have. And whenever I reached a goal, I found that I still hadn't attained that elusive thing I really wanted. Is it so necessary for everything around us to be perfect before we can move on, live our life, and experience joy?

Ron was a fifty-year-old attorney. He was organized and had an amazing ability to achieve goals. Over the previous three decades he had amassed quite a number of profitable rental properties. He leased a series of luxury cars, a new one every year. Why? "Because my car is a statement about me," he proclaimed. In a matter of three months he'd tire of each car, and, fueled by anticipation, he would plan his next lease.

When asked whether he was happy with all his financial transactions, ranging from these luxury automobiles to expensive jewelry for his wife, he said, "I feel good, but it doesn't last." With encouragement, he did some volunteer work, reduced his work hours, and struggled until he found something he was passionate about—mentoring law students. His partners at work grumbled. Ron stuck with this process anyway and discovered *time affluence*. He had more hours in which to notice and savor what was around him, and to divest himself of unnecessary possessions. He had a 1986 Corvette in various stages of repair that he got rid of, and he reaped the added benefit of his wife's approval. He donated many of his business suits. He took an inventory of his dress shirts (over one hundred) and added those to his donations. He got rid of journals, paperback books, and magazines that he had accumulated over the years. He was astounded at the amount of things he'd collected! As he decluttered, he felt a new lightness of being. He learned the power of "no." Soon he began to feel as if he was finally in control of his life. He reported increased energy levels and a significant reduction in anxiety. This was a painful process, to be sure, and he felt conflicted. His father had instilled in him a strong Protestant work ethic that allowed no room for play. The only example of self-care that he could justify was going to the gym. But at the end of the process, he felt happy.

If you get caught up in the mindset that your circumstances need to change or that you need to possess X, Y, or Z before you can be happy, it will be next to impossible to improve your situation. The truth is, we're sure to be let down by any result if we insist that happiness must look a certain way. Allow yourself time to just be.

Happiness is not a goal; it is a by-product.
~ Eleanor Roosevelt

Two Types of Motivation

Our beliefs about what will genuinely make us happy often don't address our actual needs and wants. People think that if they're wealthier, thinner, or better-looking, then everything in their life will somehow magically change and be perfect. Unfortunately, this only sets them up to be disappointed by almost every outcome. We believe that having a good job, a relationship, material possessions, or a great body will provide lasting happiness . . . until they don't.

There are two types of motivation to consider here:

1. **EXTRINSIC MOTIVATION** involves, in part, engaging in behavior to get some external reward or to avoid punishment. Think of it as doing something because someone else is providing outside encouragement or applying pressure to do it.

2. **INTRINSIC MOTIVATION**, on the other hand, involves doing something just because you like it, because it's fun in and of itself.

Unfortunately, the presence of extrinsic motivation might have the counterintuitive effect of stealing the intrinsic motivation out from under you. Though we need intrinsic motivation to enhance happiness, today it seems as if many of us are obsessed with the external, living only for the surface, and rarely digging down to deeper layers. Focusing on losing weight for cosmetic purposes rather than for health benefits or buying something to impress others and not for the actual enjoyment or practicality of the product are examples of this.

I'm reminded of a patient named Jennifer, a thirty-two-year-old tech executive who loved to buy designer clothing, shoes, and handbags, each item more extravagant than the last. She repeated this pattern with bigger-ticket items too: for instance, Jennifer would buy a Porsche 911 and then decide that she needed something even more luxurious, such as an Aston Martin. She constantly strove for excellence, not only in the quality of her possessions but also in her physical appearance. She worked out for a few hours every day, restricted her diet, and moved in high-status social circles.

Jennifer dressed to impress and modeled herself after actors who were successful and very attractive, but she still felt empty inside. She admitted that, despite all her workouts and expensive purchases, the harder she tried to acquire things to make her feel happy, the sadder she ultimately felt. She recognized that the material things she tired of so quickly were not giving her the satisfaction and fulfillment she wanted in life. She felt dissatisfied with herself but didn't know how to change. After a while, Jennifer realized that purchasing these objects and only briefly getting the results she desired meant that she needed to find some other way. Over time, she learned to do things that made her feel happy—things that didn't involve money or objects. She started spending time with "quality people" who weren't materialistic strivers like so many others she knew and had hung out with before. Instead, they were more interested in having experiences and making discoveries about themselves and the world.

As Jennifer would tell you, a sure-fire way to give yourself a life full of dissatisfaction is to keep believing that happiness will eventually come from external rewards. As with chasing the high of a drug, it's easy to become addicted to the pursuit of pleasure and joy in a detrimental way. More often than not, we look for happiness in all the wrong places until it becomes a search for our next fix.

False beliefs only clutter our minds and prevent us from fully engaging in our daily lives. Ultimately, we're held back from moving forward and improving our situations because we're *waiting* for something to occur rather than *making* something happen. If you're putting things off until you've acquired certain possessions or achieved specific circumstances, you'll probably end up waiting a very long time before making any real progress.

These false beliefs don't fix our problems or pull us out of our despair—they only cover up our negative emotions. We've all heard some variation on the phrase, "Drink your worries away"; well, this is a perfect example of a false belief, because we all know that when we try to do that, our worries don't go anywhere. They're only momentarily forgotten while we distract ourselves from our discomfort with alcohol. We're not working our way through or overcoming anything. We're merely masking it. To make matters worse, when the pain rears its ugly head again, it will be twice as unpleasant!

Want to practice true happiness?

Begin by examining your motivation before you do anything.

The (False) Belief That *This* Will Make You Happy

The handful of pursuits listed below are among the most popular that people erroneously turn to in order to find happiness. They're listed in no particular order, and are not in order of importance.

IDEALIZED RELATIONSHIPS

If you, like so many others, believe that someone else is going to provide you with complete happiness, you're setting yourself up for disaster. You eliminate any need or motivation to change your situation when you place that responsibility on another person—and when you have someone else to blame, you do.

Bear in mind that this type of deflection will keep fulfillment and happiness out of your reach. As humans, we seek meaningful relationships for support and understanding, but we also need to remember that significant and lasting connections require humility and selflessness. They become fulfilling only when we're focused on meeting the needs of a loved one in addition to our own.

I think back to the time when I first became a mother. I was so focused on my baby, Christopher, that I was able to put my physical needs on hold. Even something as insistent as hunger pangs went unnoticed because I was focusing my attention on him. At the very young age of six months, he developed asthma, and I almost lost him. I took him to the emergency room, where he was prescribed a bronchodilator. He wore a mask hooked to a machine, which I had to carry with me wherever in the world we traveled (and we traveled often). Putting

Christopher's needs first helped me as well; for the first time, I learned to say "no" to others and not give in to their demands. They weren't as important as my son, who was dependent on me for everything at that time.

Christopher was also born with a congenital cataract, which means that he is clinically blind in one eye. I recall canceling patient appointments to take him to a pediatric ophthalmologist at the University of Alberta. In the doctor's office, there was a teddy bear that was lit with bright lights, but even with the aid of those lights, Christopher was unable to identify it. It broke my heart. I've done many things over the years to compensate for his lost vision. I cut down on my workload so that I could spend more time with him, learning the infinite power of patience. And I've always treated him like an able human being, because he is. Fortunately, he no longer has asthma, but his visual impairment means that he will never be a surgeon. The way he copes with it is amazing. It's not a loss for him because it's all he knows; that's his reality. He currently volunteers and helps a blind woman. It's interesting to see how he puts his needs aside for hers. I've watched him grow into an incredible young adult, and with each decade of his life, I see new changes.

These days, I also think about my mother and how, at age eighty-nine, she's wholly dependent. She knows that she cannot live on her own anymore. A fall at her stage of life, for example, could easily result in broken limbs. I'm learning about the importance of silence, discretion, and role-reversal. The more critical issue, however, is appreciation of her humanity, of the sharp mind in the frail body.

Then there are my patients. Over the past thirty-five years, I have sometimes worked long hours because there was someone out there whose needs were more important than mine. Ironically, putting their needs ahead of my own gave me great satisfaction. I would leave my practice on a high, feeling energized because I'd made a difference, a qualitative improvement, in someone's life, if only in a minuscule way. The intrinsic satisfaction of putting my needs aside to focus on what was good for another was something I had never really been taught as a graduate student; it was only when I was in the trenches that I learned this valuable lesson, and I continue to be reminded of it to this day.

PURCHASES

We engage in this method of instant gratification, often facetiously referred to as "retail therapy," as a way to immediately boost our mood. The promise and excitement of the next shiny new toy or "comfort buy" can overpower many negative emotions. However, it isn't long before we find ourselves in a never-ending hunt for the bigger, better, faster, and stronger product that will provide us with our next adrenaline rush. In the long run, these material possessions will never satisfy us or lead to a lasting sense of happiness.

In my mid-twenties, I splurged and bought myself a wonderful dress that I thought would give me great joy because I had saved up my pennies for it. I wore it, enjoyed it, put it at the back of my closet, forgot all about it, and bought another dress later on. The same thing happened: I enjoyed it for a while and then didn't want it anymore. The dresses made me feel guilty because they had the bad manners to last, staying like unwelcome guests in my closet, so I gave them away.

I'm sure many of you experienced a similar thing while growing up—spending your money on new apparel and then saying to yourself, "Well, did I really need it? Do I still want it? Is it useful? If it is, will it last? If it's going to last, then maybe I don't want it because I know I'll get tired of it or it will fall out of fashion." I didn't realize until my thirties that the behavior I was engaging in was called *hedonic adaptation*. This is when we return to a set level of happiness after experiencing an upward or downward change in emotion. Because I didn't enjoy the things I bought for any extended period of time, I would purge my closet. Every season, I would ruthlessly go through my things and give away whatever wasn't worn. It was like hitting the reset button. Ultimately, it helped me to stop the cycle of purchasing, because I knew I would end up giving away whatever I had bought.

MONEY

Like the constant pursuit of new purchases as a way to provide happiness, the desire for money can and often does lead to a miserable place. Perhaps Zig Ziglar said it best when he observed, "Money won't make you happy . . . but everybody wants to find out for themselves." We've all heard the tragic stories about people who win the lottery and think their lives will be forever changed by the money—and, of course, they are, but often for the worse. Statistically, most big winners struggle to enjoy everyday pleasures. Their lives don't change as much as we, or they, imagined. A year after winning most of them report being as happy as they were before their unexpected good fortune, proving that money does *not* buy happiness. It may provide us with many things, such as access, status, power, and notoriety, but it can never heal our emotional wounds, bring us true love, or help us achieve long-term happiness.

According to research conducted by Dan Gilbert, the Edgar Pierce Professor of Psychology at Harvard University, our brain's prefrontal cortex has evolved over time into what he calls our *experience simulator*. Much like a flight simulator, this feature allows us to test-drive experiences in our heads before practicing them in real life. What Gilbert has found is that we experience *impact bias*, which makes our affective forecasting inaccurate—i.e., we misjudge how much happiness or sadness any given event will bring us. Moreover, we often wrongly predict that those feelings will last longer than they usually do.

I remember thinking, back when I was a poor student, "Once I graduate and start my practice, I'll be debt-free. That will make me happy." I even imagined that I would retire at age forty-five because I would have met my material goals by then. Little did I know how naïve that plan was. There were obviously other factors at play that I was blissfully unaware of at the time. In those days I was single, so I had some money saved in a "getaway account" in case misfortune occurred. It was my escape clause. Money gave me purchasing power, which made me feel independent.

What I later discovered, however, was that simply having money didn't give me the satisfaction I was looking for. Although I was able to achieve my financial goals by age forty-five, and had indeed accumulated the money I needed to retire, I found, much to my surprise, that I wasn't emotionally ready to retire at all. The truth was that I was enjoying what I was doing. I was deriving a lot of satisfaction from being a change agent for so many people. I was humbled to realize that my values had subtly changed over the years. Age forty-five came and went; so did fifty-five, and sixty-five . . . Then, when I turned sixty-nine,

When we think of income, we also have to ask ourselves, "How much is enough?" Danny Kahneman, a noted psychologist and Nobel Prize–winning economist, and Angus Deaton, also a Nobel Prize–winning economist, found that life satisfaction levels off at a yearly salary of approximately $75,000. After this point, no matter how great the additional funds, there is no increase in life satisfaction or emotional well-being. They also found that when people spent money in giving to others or to create memories, they felt happier and more satisfied. The bottom line is that once your basic needs are met, monetary increases will not bring happiness.

I decided it was time. By then I had learned that money was just a transaction, a vehicle for exchanging one thing for something else, and the feeling I got from spending money wasn't always a good one. I did, however, enjoy the intrinsic gratification of using money to do good things for other people, such as establishing a scholarship fund. Elizabeth Dunn and Mike Norton, authors of the book *Happy Money: The Science of Happier Spending*, found that people derive more satisfaction from spending money on others than they did from spending it on themselves.[2]

PHYSICAL APPEARANCE
Basing your happiness on your physical appearance is another big mistake. While it's critical to understand that a certain level

of physical discipline can improve your well-being and mood, bigger biceps or more toned thighs aren't going to have much of a long-term effect on your positive emotions. Furthermore, excessive weight training can be a potent method of avoidance when it comes to dealing with emotional problems. I love to work out; I enjoy being in the gym, hiking, and practicing yoga, among other activities. I always feel better when I stay committed to exercise, but I don't go to the gym strictly for appearance's sake. I know that exercise keeps my body and mind strong and releases endorphins that do make me feel happier—but it's a short-term hit.

JOBS

People spend so much time dreaming of the "perfect job" that they're unwilling to find contentment in anything that falls short of their high expectations. They long for a working situation with shorter hours, top pay, and limited required effort. But jobs still mean work, and that involves determination, energy, the endurance of stress, and certainly a bit of strain. You will remain unhappy in any position if you're convinced that your perfect job is right around the corner.

When I came to Edmonton in 1984, I took a hospital job that I didn't really like for a variety of reasons, the first being the routine, mechanical nature of the testing I was supposed to do. It quickly became boring, because I wasn't being challenged. I tried rearranging my office and bringing in plants, thinking that would make everything better, but it didn't help. I even moved to a bigger office in hopes that it would be warmer and more welcoming. Nothing changed. The upside of the situation was that the pay was good, and it provided me with a sense of security. Still, I struggled to make it through my first year at the hospital.

Then one day I was talking to my uncle and told him that I wanted to quit. He was dismayed and said to me, "How could you think of quitting your job when it gives you stability? You've got a pension plan, paid holidays . . . you've got everything. You're trying to create a tempest in a teacup."

Although my uncle was totally against my quitting the job, a year and a half later I resigned and opened a private practice on a shoestring budget. On paper, the hospital job appeared to be better because it provided me with financial security, but the reality of the situation was that it caused me distress, because I felt as if I weren't functioning at an optimum level. I wasn't in a flow state. The move into private practice was certainly a risk, because I knew that I could fall on my face, but it was a dream of mine. It was the most important thing in my life at the time, and fortunately, it turned out to be successful and a perfect fit. I was passionate about the work, and it fueled me. Once I'd followed my dream and was able to help patients by working with them on their stress, depression, or anxiety, I understood what real satisfaction, fulfillment, and joy are. I didn't make much money at the start, but I sure generated a lot of fulfillment, and I was tremendously proud of my work.

ACHIEVEMENTS

There is considerable value in setting and achieving short- and long-term goals. You still have to be careful, however, not to let your accomplishments define or continually fuel you. This isn't to say that there's anything wrong with setting goals and taking pride in your achievements. There's great value in both, and in allowing yourself some material rewards for all your hard work too. These incentives are essential in overcoming obstacles and pushing yourself to succeed. But be aware that at the end of the day, the only person you're competing against is yourself. I call this You-v.-You. When you approach things with that mindset, you'll always be the winner.

DISTRACTIONS

Often, when we're unhappy or feeling down, we explore various methods of escape and distraction, such as bingeing a new series on a streaming service, going out for an evening, or planning a trip. Although a weekend getaway may serve as a much-needed change of scenery, your problems and unhappiness will still be waiting for you when you return home. Confronting issues is always better than running away from them.

Distractions are a wonderful way to avoid core issues, but they're not much more than Band-Aids. I'd rather you grit your teeth, pull the Band-Aid off, and deal with the wound that's festering beneath. Instead of seeking solace in surface distractions, it might be better to deal with the underlying issues that are really bothering you in an assertive way. We sometimes want to practice denial and ignore issues by pursuing other things. We might even have good intentions, choosing healthier diversions such as going to the gym, but on our way there we end up running into a friend and sitting down for a drink. Or we might go down a rabbit hole on the Internet—an addictive distraction if ever there was one—instead of dealing with what's really causing our distress. Although you feel good by visiting a friend, occupying your mind with social media, shopping, getting away for a spa weekend, or whatever else it is that you choose to distract yourself with, in the end, these are only temporary fixes.

Sometimes the pursuit of distractions is really just a pre-occupation with new possibilities, which can lead to our disregarding the happiness we already have. More often, though, pursuing distractions is a conscious decision not to deal with our issues. On their own, distractions aren't bad, but it's important to realize why you're behaving this way. It's okay to take a break from your problems by separating yourself from them—whether that involves a weekend in the mountains or whatever it is you do to get distance and clarity—as long as it's done with the intent of coming back and dealing with those problems. You might go away for a few days, rejuvenate, and then come back and say to yourself, "This job sucks! I need a different one" instead of staying with the same old routine. You may also take some time away from a dysfunctional relation-ship and come back and say, "Now I need to deal with this. I need to separate."

Overall, if you attempt to force happiness through one of these ways—idealized relationships, purchases, money, phys-ical appearance, jobs, achievements, or distractions—it will never be lasting and genuine. In focusing our efforts on any of these areas, we satisfy the beliefs we hold in our minds about what will make us happy—in the short run, anyway. But each boost they provide is just a temporary emotion. As time passes, our expectations will change and our feelings will shift. Even-tually, we'll need to reassess our pursuit of these means, and in so doing, our beliefs about what will make us happy will change too.

The Hedonic Treadmill

So, what happens when we work hard to acquire and achieve the things our minds led us to believe would make us happy, only to discover that we still feel almost the same—or, worse, completely unfulfilled?

As mentioned, our tendency to rapidly return to our previous emotional state despite positive or negative life changes is known as hedonic adaptation. It's also aptly called the *hedonic treadmill,* because its cyclical nature lands you right back where you started.

The majority of us are poor predictors of how long attaining or achieving external rewards will make us happy. No matter how greatly we may have previously envisioned how a material purchase or a specific achievement will alter our life, it's usually not as good or as bad as we forecast.

We've all had the experience of saving money to eventually buy something we desperately wanted. The sense of excitement that comes with the purchase is typically a satisfying rush. Unfortunately, the euphoria doesn't last forever (although on some level we may expect it to). The intense emotion eventually fades, and the sense of joy rapidly diminishes. The *newness* wears off, and before we know it, we're at the same point emotionally as where we began. As we move forward, we adapt to the feeling of satisfaction, and eventually reach a juncture where we're no longer fulfilled by the same things. Though we may believe that the more we get of something, the more we'll enjoy it, this usually turns out to be false. The ensuing situation becomes the new normal and stops bringing us the happiness we expect.

Our baseline expectations are continually set and reset as we move through life. Ideally, this paves the way for a gradual and continual push forward. But what happens when the bar is suddenly set too high and outpaces our natural advancement? We become unsatisfied and unfulfilled. For example, if you're awarded a pay raise of 5 percent at your job, the next time you'll need an even higher percentage to be satisfied, because your baseline expectation of what will make you happy will be different.

Even if we were able to acquire and achieve everything we currently desire, we still wouldn't be sustainably happy. We've all heard about or even met someone we believed had it all only to find out that they still thought it wasn't enough. Once our baseline expectations are fulfilled, we get comfortable, and eventually a new void is created, accompanied by dissatisfaction and disconnection. We can check all of the boxes—have a great job, an expensive house, a supportive family, money in the bank—and still think to ourselves, "I'm just not happy, and I don't know why."

So, the next time around, we set our goal for satisfaction and happiness even higher—and by setting the happiness bar at such a high level, we make ourselves miserable when we fail to meet the goal.

It's essential to remind ourselves that no matter what we achieve or acquire, we will eventually adapt to our situation. This is why we have to be careful not to overestimate the emotional impact of the things we purchase or the favorable conditions we experience. It's only a matter of time before the reality of a new daily grind sets in and brings with it new obstacles and challenges.

Jack was a forty-five-year-old retired owner of a retail franchise. "Why aren't I happy?" he wondered. He had achieved financial freedom, didn't have to work, and had a wife and a happy family. He expressed feelings of emptiness: "I'm dead inside; just going through the motions. I don't care for sex anymore." Jasmine, his wife, began to feel that she was unattractive.

Over the next six months, Jack journeyed inward. The process awakened in him some renewed passion and drive. He reconnected with Jasmine and found an avocation by becoming a tennis coach. With time and this pursuit, he came alive again. The journey was painful at times; Jack felt conflicted and guilty for feeling blue. "On paper, I've just fulfilled the American dream. I've made it financially," he told me. But he stayed with the process and gradually experienced clarity. Work had always given him a sense of purpose, and he'd linked his self-esteem to his job so deeply that his net worth became his self-worth. How often do we all fall into that trap? I know I did. Early in my career, I had a burning desire to be of service to my patients and to do well financially. Guess what? At forty-five I had achieved my goals and could enjoy the luxury of choice. I chose to work from there on out because it was fulfilling. The bills were being paid, but the desire and the passion were what continued to fuel me more than the money. I couldn't retire, because this was way too much fun! And it was mentally challenging too. I was living out my values. As I worked with Jack, he began to have similar thoughts. Have you ever thought about what you would do if you retired? What would give you passion or a sense of contribution? Knowing the answer to this question is all part of living a happy life.

When Being Too Positive Is a Negative

In addition to putting too much importance on injecting happiness into everything we do, pushing ourselves to be overly optimistic can also distract us from directly addressing the causes of our discontentment. Although a healthy mind requires a positive outlook, when we push ourselves into an exceedingly upbeat mindset, we're only moving into a state of denial. Instead of working through the tough emotions we may be facing, we often repress them and create situations to distract us. By not taking the time to deal with the roots of our negative emotions, we miss the opportunity to confront, manage, and overcome our suffering.

When we spend our time pursuing what we assume will bring us happiness, we just cause more problems for ourselves and add to our sadness and disappointment with life. This never-ending hunt for joy turns out to be nothing more than a diversion that negatively impacts our psyche. When we fall short and don't meet the requirements that we set for our happiness, we provide ourselves more reasons to be unhappy. For example, if we decide happiness will ensue once we lose ten pounds and we instead end up losing only five, there's a letdown. In attempting to steer ourselves in the direction of happiness, we've only added to our suffering. In short, we've turned a positive into a negative.

Psychologist Dr. Iris Mauss, who has done extensive research on happiness, has provided scientific evidence that the more value we put on maintaining what she refers to as the *optimist's mindset*, the less happy we are. We become so caught up in evaluating our lives that we never allow ourselves to fully engage in the present. By determining our daily existence to be unenjoyable and unfulfilling, we add to our displeasure—because whenever we fall short of our ultimate goals, the ensuing sadness feels justified. Our pursuit of happiness fails to bring us any joy at all when we get stuck in this mindset.

So, it seems that experiencing too much optimism or happiness is probably just as harmful in the long run as experiencing too little. The real goal, I believe, is to find a state of emotional balance where we're just as present and available to deal with sadness, anxiety, and anger as we are to experience positive emotions.

Happiness Self-Test

Respond to each of the following statements with either Yes or No:

1. Am I less than satisfied with my life?
2. Is there something I would like to change?
3. Am I anxious at times?
4. Do I experience any trouble sleeping?
5. Do I sometimes wish I could [fill in the blank]?
6. Do I want to improve my feeling of wellness?
7. Am I easily irritated or frustrated by everyday events?
8. Am I often despondent?
9. Do I sometimes feel like I'm missing something in my life?
10. Do I want to feel happier in general?

© Joan. Z. Neehall, PhD, R. Psych.

chapter two

COMPARE AT YOUR OWN RISK

Comparison is the thief of joy.
—Theodore Roosevelt

Comparison is a basic human impulse. It's more important to try to understand its origin and evaluate why, how, and when we're comparing ourselves than it is to actually see how we match up. Are these comparisons surfacing as a result of our search for happiness? Do we gravitate toward such thoughts to help deal with underlying unhappiness or stress?

Just as we make the mistake of looking to external sources in our search for happiness, we also lean on unfavorable comparisons that can be incredibly destructive to our well-being. Society conditions us to hold ourselves up to others using a constructed concept of what is considered "successful." There's always pressure to measure up. And when we're unhappy in life, our insecurity and fear can motivate us to look to others to reinforce our beliefs about how the world works. By and large, though, these frequent comparisons only make matters worse and eat up valuable time we could be spending on beneficial activities. It puts us in a holding pattern as we assess and reassess how successful or unsuccessful we may be at any given time. The bottom line is that no matter what we do to try to increase our happiness, falling into excessive comparisons can easily rob us of it. Worrying about what we have or don't have relative to others ultimately adds to the amount of stress and anxiety we carry in our lives.

Comparisons can serve as one way to measure our observations, progress, and satisfaction with life, but they're not the *only* way. At their foundation, they're supposed to be instantaneous assessments to identify threats and help us take necessary measures to protect ourselves. We process our observations of people and our surroundings and then make decisions accordingly. We compare things by a variety of distinctions, such as their cost, outward appearance, or level of performance. We typically compare ourselves to others in terms of finances, body type, wardrobe, travel experiences, talents, and house size, which, more often than not, leads to a lot of "should-ing." For example:

"I should have a bigger house."

"I should have a more expensive car."

"I should be in better shape."

We utilize comparisons not only to place things in context but also to assign a value of good or bad to them, something psychologists refer to as *valence*. Determining whether something is harmful or not is key to our survival—and in some situations, an ability to come up with valence information quickly can mean the difference between life and death.

Comparing can also act as a natural appraisal that helps us take into consideration how others see us so we can develop a sense of who we are in society. But by routinely dwelling on personal or material shortcomings, we keep feeling that we've fallen short of our expectations and have made too many wrong choices.

It's vital to note that if you already suffer from low self-esteem, then comparisons of any kind are likely to make you feel even worse. By focusing on what others have, you place heavy emphasis on what's missing from your life. It's destructive to set high standards for ourselves and then feel unhappy and unaccomplished when we don't reach our goals. Comparison triggers feelings of inadequacy and frustration, which eat away at our confidence and sense of gratitude. Unhappy people make more frequent social judgments and are more emotionally affected by the contrast than those who are happy.

Naturally, when confronted by others and exposed to new situations, we automatically and spontaneously make observations. But when we fall into creating unfavorable comparisons and focus on what we lack in life, we run into a lot of trouble. Today, it seems like we've become obsessed with where we stand in relation to other people. Social media certainly adds to this, and I'll address that later in this chapter.

When we're always concerned with comparing ourselves to others, we aren't focusing our energy on self-improvement and developing our capabilities. We stop appreciating who we are and what we've been blessed with in life. Every one of us has a lot to offer, and the moment we forget this is the moment we lose track of our gratitude for what we have.

Fueled by Discontent

We notice when something is different and naturally compare our experience or circumstances to those of others when
it comes to education, appearance, finances, occupation, and
plenty of other categories. But we're also motivated to make
additional comparisons by general fear, insecurity, and our
egos, which force us to focus on the surface instead of what lies
deeper. If we aren't feeling good, we tend to zero in on ways we
can at least *appear* good. This is most often a result of our egos
prompting us to concentrate on surface-level matters.

In contrast, I'm sure you've noticed at one time or another
that people who are content and fulfilled don't feel the need
to regularly consider what they have or don't have. But in frequently checking to see what others have achieved in their lives,
you only make yourself more uneasy and insecure about your
accomplishments. And just as we've seen in assessing our levels
of happiness, setting too-high expectations of where we should
be in relation to others keeps us on a path toward inevitable
misery.

We encounter trouble when we hold on to our notions of
ideal situations and outcomes. If life turns into a never-ending
quest to be a better version of yourself, then you'll continually
be left feeling depressed and unsatisfied. How could you ever
be content?

Are comparisons helping you get to where you need to be
in life?

Are you happy for other people's success, or are you jealous?

We sometimes get so lost in other people's lives that we end
up forgetting to be satisfied with our own.

Ali was a forty-five-year-old part-time employee at a major news service, where her duties included sorting and delivering mail. She was married to Bob, an entrepreneur who had two sons from a prior relationship. Ali had two sons from a previous marriage as well, and their blended family was not without its challenges. Ali held a BA, which she'd earned while married to Bob and co-parenting their four sons, yet she constantly compared herself to other women and fell short in her assessment. The other women were more attractive, intelligent, and successful, from her point of view. She questioned whether Bob still found her attractive after decades together. She also felt as if her friends used her for favors, not necessarily because they enjoyed her company. If she asked for help in return, it was never forthcoming. Life for her seemed like a constant stream of heavy responsibilities. She recalled having to care for her five younger siblings while her mother worked two jobs. She confided that she felt guilty for working only part-time and for not keeping a tidy house, despite the fact that Bob's job involved working in an oil field and dragging in muddy work boots—or that his six employees did the same! With some guidance from me, Ali started identifying her needs and began negotiating with Bob, her friends, and her children. It took a long time for her to stop making unfair comparisons, but ultimately she did. Whenever she would catch herself slipping back into her old way of thinking, she practiced gratitude, which helped stop the comparisons. She found more efficient ways to do things for her loved ones, which left her with some extra time to care for herself. For instance, she set a thirty-minute timer to limit how long she spent in the kitchen preparing dinner each night, and during the holidays she ordered some of her family's favorite foods instead of making them herself. She even asked Bob to take her to Las Vegas for a getaway weekend, which he did. While they were there, Bob bought her a purse. Ali's initial reaction was to feel guilty about it because of all the money they'd already spent on travel and accommodations. "Do I deserve this?" she asked. It took a while for her to receive gifts, accept compliments, and give herself permission to occasionally do nothing but relax. She ultimately learned to value her time whether she brought home a large paycheck or not. Her tendency to be self-effacing disappeared, but not without constant vigilance. Comparisons to others had been so automatic for her that she once caught herself doing it 150 times in one day.

Types of Comparisons

To make sense of the constant observations and comparisons we make of the actions and circumstances around us, social psychologists have classified three principal types of comparisons: *counterfactual*, *temporal*, and *social*.

Counterfactual comparisons compare "what is" to "what might have been."

Temporal comparisons compare the way things are right now to how they used to be or may one day become. For example, if you envision the person you were five, ten, or even fifteen years ago, what thoughts come to mind? You were probably a much different person then than you are today. Ideally, we would think of ourselves as being on an upward trajectory of personal advancement throughout our lives. This isn't always the case, however.

Social comparisons compare you to other people. In my opinion, they cause us to feel the most inadequate and probably present the biggest problems in our lives because a large part of our perceptions about the world are based on them. It's so easy to get caught up in this type of comparison, as we're continually bombarded with images of impossible standards to live up to. We encounter them every day in magazines, television, movies, and especially social media.

Our minds naturally gravitate toward observed differences, but additional problems rear their ugly heads when we start to routinely identify similarities with those to whom we feel inferior or superior, or when the differences we focus on are with people we admire. The tendency is then to feel less than and critical of ourselves, and thus we're made unhappy and discontent.

<hr>

Be thankful for what you have;
you'll end up having more.
If you concentrate on what you don't have,
you will never, ever have enough.
~ Oprah Winfrey

<hr>

How you ultimately process these comparisons determines whether they'll make you feel more positive or more negative about your current situation. Each of these comparisons is vital to our psychology in that they represent a function of the brain's natural response to danger. If we look at how we react to the problems we encounter, there are two main options: change your mind about a situation or change the situation itself. One type of reaction focuses on the mind and emotion, while the other focuses on action and behavior. So, you can either choose to reframe the experience and think of it differently or take the necessary action to fix the problem.

Social Media

Before the COVID-19 pandemic, which we'll discuss at length in chapter 10, I had so many patients who would spend an incredible amount of time on social media, a solitary activity that typically led to greater feelings of disconnection and social isolation.

So how did we let it get to that point?

Before the advent of social media, we typically found out about other people's good news through conversation, word of mouth, the local newspaper, or maybe through an alumni newsletter. Today, however, we're exposed to a constant stream of people's personal information that our minds must process. We have access to images of others at all times, everywhere. And as unrealistic as these images may be—their subjects have often been Photoshopped, airbrushed, or even surgically altered—they still seem to drive current human behavior and determine what's accepted as the social norm. In short, the social media we confront every day is like social comparison on steroids.

Although our focus on comparison should fade considerably as we get older and more mature, it seems that the rise of social media has made this close to impossible. Many of us may have initially joined these platforms as a way to remain in contact with the people who are important to us, but over time they've taken on another purpose. Social media will undoubtedly connect or reconnect you to people you value, but it will also throw images in your face of situations and things you don't and maybe will never have in life. FOMO (fear of missing out) is real and it's damaging, because people experience rejection in real time. Scrolling through posts to see what others are up to has become a constant reminder of the possessions you *don't* own, the vacations you *haven't* taken, the parties you *haven't* attended, and the people you *aren't* privileged to know.

It's easy to forget that the picture social media presents is heavily skewed. That's why I refer to Facebook as "Put on a Happy Facebook"!

Comparing ourselves to others' posts can often leave us feeling sad and depressed. It can also lead us to such thoughts as:

I'm not talented, educated, attractive, or wealthy enough.

I'm embarrassed by my job.

I'm unable to afford wonderful vacations.

I'm unable to indulge in creature comforts and expensive meals.

I haven't achieved as much as others have.

I don't have good friends to spend time with.

I'm lonely.

It's important to remember that most posts are carefully edited and filtered representations of people's realities. They're generated to accomplish one thing: to make the person posting look as if they're living life to the fullest, whether they actually are or not. All too often, however, they remind us that we're not living our lives to the fullest. The photo of the gorgeous craft cocktail someone is having with dinner lets us know that we're not enjoying a cocktail of our own. The video of a coworker's brand-new sports car reminds us that we, by contrast, are still eking out payments on the family car. By getting caught up in these comparisons, we relinquish our power over our own situations.

These representations of your Facebook friends' existence are, in many ways, engineered to make others feel jealous and downcast. As you scroll through their feed, you're inundated by an incredible number of highlights and achievements. How can you possibly not be jealous of such experiences? People rarely post about their failures, and so the drastic juxtaposition of these sparkling images with the reality of our actual everyday lives can make things seem so much worse. If you find yourself feeling depressed, you probably don't need to be barraged with photographs and videos of excited and smiling people enjoying a lifestyle different from your own.

So when you go on social media and look at how everybody else is living, consider whether it's making you feel better or worse than before you logged in. Do you see a goal you're inspired to achieve as you scroll around? Or is it something unattainable that instead makes you miserable? Sure, social media can be fun and entertaining, but not if it makes you feel downtrodden and anxious.

When we take a moment to clear our minds and think about the situation, we can consider whether we care deep down about the content people share, or whether repeated exposure to these things is *causing* us to think that we should care about them. For the most part, there's no reason for us to be concerned with much of what we're exposed to on social media. After all, what's the personal benefit of knowing what your friends have just purchased, let alone what they're eating for breakfast, lunch, and dinner? Honestly, very little.

Comparison Quiz

—Do you spend the majority of your time comparing yourself to others?

—Where do your expectations originate? Are they from your thoughts or from outside sources?

—Who do you compare yourself to most often? Family members? Friends? Colleagues? Strangers?

—Are you able to feel satisfied with yourself without receiving feedback from others?

Genuinely amazing, even miraculous things are going to happen to other people no matter what you think, say, or do. That's simply the way it is.

Although numbers of followers and likes may appear to provide proof of a person's value, these figures are incredibly misleading and ultimately have little or nothing to do with one's actual self-worth.

Young people, especially teenagers, are particularly susceptible to seeking valuation on social media because their brains are sensitive to social rewards during the adolescent transition. When we feel that we're receiving positive feedback and attention from others, our brains release dopamine into our systems. The same effect can take place when we compare ourselves to people we admire or respect and find similarities. It's very easy to become addicted to this mental and physical reward over time, no matter how old we may be.

Even worse, social media also presents us with a personal score, a numerical value of our status on the imaginary social media scoreboard. Yes, the experiences we consider essential are being graded! We see this in the number of our LinkedIn connections, Facebook likes, Instagram hearts, and Twitter followers. We're even more disappointed with our overall status when we put up posts that fail to garner as much enthusiasm as other people's. But have we considered what response would be satisfying?

How many likes is enough? Twenty? One hundred? One thousand?

Ask yourself: Is it healthy to absorb other people's triumphs on a minute-by-minute basis? How about on even an hourly or daily basis? Take a look at your online activities, the frequency with which you log in, and the length of time you spend on social media platforms and decide what is the right amount for your situation, and what will be most beneficial to your mindset.

Janine was a thirty-year-old fitness consultant. She was recovering from a serious car accident in which she sustained a broken rib and multiple knee injuries. She was in constant pain. Her main concern was that she was disappointing her more than ten thousand social media followers by her inability to continue posting videos of her workout regime. The more she agonized about this, the more her anxiety increased.

Several months later she was able to look at her car accident and its deleterious aftermath as a temporary setback. She visualized herself as an ingenious survivor and used her long months of rehabilitation as an opportunity to respect her body, practice mindfulness, and reevaluate her priorities. Although it was a challenge, Janine practiced "mental gymnastics" in lieu

---

Conducting a Digital Detox

So, how should we deal with the feelings of inadequacy social media brings about in our lives? An excellent place to start is to assess your lists of connections, followers, and friends and delete the people whose posts and photos don't add anything positive to your day. There is, of course, another, more drastic option: you can literally and figuratively "shut it down." You have the ability to schedule breaks for yourself or even turn your phone off for specific periods each day or week. Don't compare yourself to others—compare yourself to who you were yesterday, last week, or last month. Are you progressing on your own merits? Spend less time self-analyzing and more time doing what you do best: being yourself.

---

of physical workouts and took the opportunity to share uplifting posts with her followers. "This was one of the best times of my life," she wrote about engaging her psychological immune system in order to reduce her stress and anxiety.

* * *

The big question about how people behave
is whether they've got an Inner Scorecard
or an Outer Scorecard. It helps if you can
be satisfied with an Inner Scorecard.
~ Warren Buffett

* * *

Celebrity Culture

While the people to whom we compare ourselves tend to be those in our circles with whom we most closely identify, we can also fixate on people well outside of our personal orbit. In addition to those of our friends, family, and other acquaintances, we also envy the lives of celebrities and public figures. We admire their work and follow their social media posts, where they often promote products.

So, why does everyone want to be a celebrity? Because they look like they have it all!

But having it all isn't always what it appears to be, and in no way does it ensure happiness.

Consider, for example, something called *confirmation bias.* A celebrity looks like he or she is losing weight by following a strict diet or taking a new supplement, and the dynamism and influence of that person makes their testimonial seem powerful and compelling. Their image supports the apparent correlation between the regimen and the weight loss—even if, on a conscious level, we ignore the testimonial.

Some speculative research in the context of evolution points to an explanation for the emulation of celebrity culture. The suggestion is that there was historically an advantage in comparing ourselves to and following people with prestige. Early humans might have assumed that their higher-ups' status was the result of having useful skills or talents, such as being excellent hunters, food collectors, or whatever else was essential for life at that time.

Comparing and copying, in this case, would have been a survival technique that then became a genetic predisposition

Quiz: Celebrities and Me

Respond to each of the following statements with either Yes or No:

1. I buy pop-culture magazines only occasionally— and just to skim through.
2. I look at and/or read pop-culture magazines when in a waiting room.
3. I enjoy watching awards shows, mostly to see what the celebrities are wearing.
4. I (sometimes or often) discuss celebrities and their behavior with friends.
5. I (sometimes or often) think it's unfair that celebrities are so wealthy when the average person is not.
6. I admit to being (even a little) jealous of everything celebrities seem to have—opulent homes, extravagant lifestyles, fancy clothes, and so forth.
7. I (sometimes or often) watch television shows about celebrities.
8. I admire particular celebrities for their positive positions on humanity and the environment.
9. I admire—even envy—the beautiful appearances of celebrities.
10. I tend to assign particular personality traits to celebrities based on what I see or hear.

If you answered Yes to more than half of these statements, well, you (like so many of us) are influenced by celebrity culture.

to copy those deemed more esteemed than oneself. Where originally this might have been a life-and-death decision, today it appears to be more of a coping mechanism: the brain associates celebrity success with our adaptive behaviors. We don't need to be like them to survive, but we *want* to be like them nevertheless.

You may feel that you're in total control and not at all influenced by celebrities. But if you take the time to evaluate your situation, you may discover a different response.

Looks Matter

Cosmetic surgery has become increasingly widespread in popular culture. People are altering their faces and/or bodies in different ways. Without celebrity culture, such an uptick would not exist. For example, many people will go to great lengths to attain full lips similar to Angelina Jolie's, a round derrière like Kim Kardashian's, or the abs of Jennifer Lopez.

And this isn't just a trend among women—cosmetic surgery among men is on the rise as well. It's usually motivated by the desire to enhance or improve a feature either connected to power or commonly classified as sexually attractive.[1] Rhinoplasty, double eyelid surgery, and face-lifts are designed to help men look fitter, leaner, younger, and more "masculine."

A significant amount of research has shown that conventionally attractive people tend to receive advantages in our society, and celebrity culture certainly leverages that. The public has come to believe that, because "looks matter," human beings should invest personal resources in "improvement" of their appearances. Celebrities set the standard and create the drive, and beauty companies repeatedly remind us that to look like the celebrities, we should do as they do.

Consider the plight of doctors who are asked by patients to duplicate a celebrity's appearance through cosmetic surgery, only for the result to fall short of the patient's expectations. This is an example of the social comparative phenomenon; on some level, most people know that it's unrealistic to hope to attain that image, but nevertheless they scramble to attempt it.

Right in Your Face

Celebrity influence still permeates society even when it's widely accepted that the person is compromised on some level. We're all aware of celebrity doctors who receive unfavorable press questioning the validity of their advice and/or the products they promote on TV, yet they continue to influence people. This is primarily due to what is known as *availability bias*, in which there is the tendency to let readily available and easily accessible examples of something affect reasoning and decision making.[2] The prevalence of certain personalities can often trump any rationale when it comes to the choices we make.

Using Comparison for Good

Although overreliance on unfavorable comparisons can lead us down a path to unhappiness and disconnection, other people's good news can also make us feel inspired. It can lead us to further understand who we truly are and help us identify our strengths and weaknesses. So, as awful as comparisons may seem when we continually engage in them, they aren't *all* bad. In many ways, it can be beneficial to productively measure ourselves against others. We know that being overly competitive can lead to feelings of jealousy, but why not flip the script and instead use other people's achievements as inspiration to pursue your own life goals? Social contrast has long helped people identify their natural talents and best qualities, allowing them to thrive.

Also, by occasionally acknowledging that your skills and abilities are a level above those of others, you strengthen your self-esteem; and observing and appreciating other people's elevated talents and accomplishments can sometimes provide us with the strong desire needed to improve our own skills. And if, by chance, we realize that we *don't* have a talent for something, that can be a valuable lesson as well, saving us time and effort that we can put toward the pursuit of something else more suited to us.

There are certain people in our society after whom it's good to model ourselves—people with particular skills, ways of being, and personality traits that we would like to emulate. Among those behaviors and traits are compassion and understanding.

Margaret, a woman in her late sixties, said that she would like to be able to exude the confidence of Meryl Streep or Helen Mirren as she entered her next decade. She explained that both women are beautiful, mature, and seem able to hold their own in public and also in private. Margaret had started to emulate what she perceived as their poise, and by osmosis, it became part of her persona. She was able to be more confident when she had to speak in public and more self-assured when she went to cocktail parties and social events. To take better care of her body, she started going to the gym more frequently. Not only did her appearance improve, but her health and range of movement did as well.

Another example would be Beverly, a forty-nine-year-old owner of several day care centers. She had been drawn to her profession because she loved helping others, but as the demands of her business grew, she found herself more involved with paperwork than people. She was an admirer of the late Mother Teresa. She said, "I'd like to act like she did. I'd like to have compassion for people. I want to be able to serve others with a smile on my face and to put my needs last." When I asked if there was anything else about Mother Teresa that she liked, she mentioned her ability to be humble and to give untiringly. Beverly perceived Mother Teresa as very generous, caring, and authentic. She actively began to emulate those qualities, and in doing so, she reported increased life satisfaction. Her interpersonal relationships improved, as did her relationship with herself. As a result, she felt younger, more energetic, and more gratified overall.

Then there are the examples of people who have survived near-fatal motor vehicle accidents, the loss of a limb, or a debilitating illness and worked hard to recover because they modeled the determination of someone they saw in the media who had endured a similar experience. After adopting the same kind of driven mindset, these people have reported experiencing more confidence in themselves and an increased ability to cope with and rebound from their physical challenges. When John, who lost the use of his dominant arm in an accident, arrived in my office, his concern was that he'd lost quite a bit in his life. He felt that he was a failure, and that, beyond feeling restrained in his activities, no one would want to become involved with him in a romantic relationship. John was thirty-three years old at the time.

"Do you know of anyone who's been in a similar situation or lost the use of a limb and was able to survive and become a role model?" I asked.

"Terry Fox," was his immediate reply.

Terry lost his leg in a battle with cancer and later decided to run coast to coast in Canada to help raise awareness and money for cancer research. He inspired so many people that the Terry Fox Run became an annual event. "What is it about Terry Fox that you admire?" I asked John.

"His tenacity," John said immediately. "I also like his courage and the fact that he didn't get so self-absorbed that all he could think about was what he'd lost. He didn't hide it and went on to run for a cause."

Before sharing this thought with me, John had hidden his prosthesis and wouldn't let anyone close to him for fear that they would notice it and reject him. He saw it as a personal defect. With his work as a computer programmer, he was relatively isolated from other people, which didn't help the situation. His interpersonal contact was almost nonexistent. But more and more, he began to emulate the qualities he perceived Terry Fox as having—the courage to be himself, to disclose who he was, and to transform his loss into a gain for other people.

So, how did John do this? For starters, he revealed his prosthesis and started volunteering in the orthopedic division at the University of Alberta Hospital. He began looking at his prosthesis as an asset instead of a handicap, and challenged himself to transform it into something that was life-affirming. It was a difficult process, but Terry Fox proved to be an effective model for John.

Today, the athletes participating in the Invictus Games, an international adaptive sports competition founded by Prince Harry, the Duke of Sussex, in 2014, have become an additional source of inspiration for many like John. These wounded, ill, or injured armed services personnel and veterans demonstrate their strength of mind and body, exceptional athletic skills, and, in many cases, mastery of their prostheses through sport.

Hal, a sixty-five-year-old university professor, suffered from chronic intermittent depression. He talked about how he felt so exhausted and disconnected from other people that at times it was hard for him to even dress himself and go to work. Teaching had become more of a chore than a joy, especially when he was experiencing a depressive episode. He would isolate himself from others, which caused him to feel even more alienated. Over the course of a lifetime, this behavior had cost him two marriages.

When I asked him who he admired, Hal replied, "Winston Churchill."

I asked, "Are you aware that Winston Churchill suffered from depression?"

"Yep. But his bad-dog days weren't half as bad as mine."

"Well, what do you think Winston Churchill looked like when he was depressed? And can you sort out how he managed to function in spite of his depression?"

Hal went home to think about my questions, and then came back the following week with some insights. "Well, he just soldiered on. Maybe I just need to soldier on too," he told me.

I knew that Churchill was infamous for his temper, so I asked, "And be bad-tempered too?"

Hal laughed. "I'm learning to bite my tongue."

Incidentally, Hal was a prolific writer who'd published several blind-reviewed journal articles, and he was beloved by his students. But when he was depressed, he perceived none of this. He confided in me that he felt as if he were sliding downward through a dark tunnel with no end in sight. When Hal motivated himself to emulate Winston Churchill and soldier on, however, he was able to begin functioning in a more meaningful way. He realized that depression didn't have to last a lifetime.

In each of these examples, the person was able to transform loss into gain and to home in on their skill set in order to sharpen it, to give themselves a sense of empowerment because of what they could do. Essentially, they were able to adopt the "Yes I can" model instead of the "Yes I can, but . . ." model. The concept of choice became very important to them when they realized they could choose to be more like the notable people they admired.

If we continually remind ourselves of what we don't like about our lives, we'll find it very difficult to progress and achieve any of our goals. By accepting the fact that we may not be especially skilled in certain areas or possess certain mindsets, we can turn our attention to the talents we do possess. Remember that all of us are unique, so why are we trying to be something we're not? We're all different, and that's perfectly okay. It's much more empowering to embrace who we are. You will always be able to find someone who does something better than you do, but don't forget that you're better than anyone else on the planet at being yourself.

***

Be yourself; everyone else is already taken.
~ Oscar Wilde

chapter three

LONELINESS

Find company within yourself and you'll never spend a day alone.
Find love within yourself and you'll never have a lonely day.
—Connor Chalfant

When we pursue happiness too adamantly, play the constant comparison game, and hold ourselves to unrealistic goals for achievement and success, we eventually arrive at a place of isolation and loneliness. Dr. Iris Mauss conducted a study that found the more people value happiness, the lonelier they felt on a daily basis. According to Dr. Mauss, "If you want to be happy, you may be more likely to focus on yourself, and that can have negative effects on your social networks and your social connections."[1] Focusing on our personal needs and wants too often can send us down a rabbit hole of loneliness and social isolation. In our pursuit of happiness we can end up concentrating mostly on ourselves and shutting others out, allowing our social networks and connections with others to crumble.

Although the terms *loneliness* and *social isolation* are often used interchangeably, it's essential to point out that they actually refer to *different* states of being. Loneliness is defined by a person's level of satisfaction with his or her perceived connectedness, while isolation refers to a person who has infrequent contact with others and possesses few or no friends. One can be quantified while the other cannot—and this is why loneliness is a subjective experience that makes addressing its prevalence very challenging. After all, we're talking about our perceptions and feelings.

Isolation can be caused by a wide range of situations, such as the tragic loss of a loved one, a change to a new school, a transition in the workplace, an introduction to a new social circle of people who don't share your curiosities, or the lack of a current love interest in your life. And as we all are aware by now, it can also be perpetuated by physical-distancing measures and stay-at-home orders implemented by federal, state/province, and local governments as a means of protecting the most vulnerable in our society during crises such as the COVID-19 pandemic.

Times of disconnection will occur no matter how much you worry or what you attempt to do to prevent them. What's important are how often they arise and how long they linger. Once we've achieved an understanding of the kind of loneliness we're experiencing, then we can move to address it. These feelings can be brought on by several different circumstances that fall mainly into two categories:

Situational loneliness temporarily surfaces as you go about your life and attempt to create new connections with the world around you.

Chronic loneliness repeatedly occurs for extended periods but never lessens or subsides.

If situational loneliness is ignored, it can quickly turn into chronic loneliness. The longer you put off trying to remedy the problem of connecting with others, the more difficult it will be to eventually dig yourself out of that hole, move forward, and recover. Before you know it, you'll find yourself more and more reluctant to reach out for help. That's why it's important to keep a close eye on your loneliness whenever it surfaces and act to change your situation as early as you can.

Loneliness is something that can manifest in many different forms, such as anxiety, depression, and disconnection. It accompanies a feeling that you aren't present in your life. Based on my thirty-five years of professional experience, I would estimate that 90 percent of the patients in my clinical practice suffer from loneliness. So, although the term *epidemic* is usually reserved for infectious diseases or severe addictions, it undoubtedly fits here, given the 2018 estimates that loneliness affects approximately sixty million Americans! Typically, when we hear the phrase "public health crisis," our thoughts quickly turn to vital national issues such as opioid addiction, vaping, obesity, or, more recently, novel viruses. But the new epidemic of loneliness fits right in with these afflictions and, fortunately, is beginning to garner the widespread attention it deserves.

According to pre-coronavirus research, rates of loneliness have *doubled* over the last fifty years in the United States.[2] Almost 50 percent of the people surveyed reported feeling alone or left out, and had also experienced isolation. They said their relationships weren't meaningful. The study determined that those born after approximately 1995—a group often referred to as Generation Z—are considered the loneliest generation in recent times (and Millennials are right up there too). Loneliness doesn't discriminate. It's a profound issue that affects people no matter their gender, race, ethnicity, or geographic location.

A drastic rise in levels of loneliness has been making headlines not only in the US but also in other countries around the world. The negative implications of loneliness are felt regardless of the culture in which it occurs. One study found that over 23 percent of adults in England and 9 percent of adults in Japan reported "always or often" feeling lonely.[3] England has gone so far as to essentially create a "Minister of Loneliness" to combat the rise of social isolation in the country. Certainly the COVID-19 pandemic has exacerbated the problem.

At one time or another, however, we've all experienced the feeling of being left out or disconnected from the world around us. We typically have an expectation of a certain level of social interaction in our minds, and it's easy to experience loneliness when our degree of actual interaction falls short. Periodically, everyone experiences disconnection for a time. Disconnection at either the individual (intrapersonal) or social (interpersonal) levels will result in unhappiness. The extent to which we respond to isolation or disconnection varies from individual to individual, depending on our tolerance for disconnection and our degree of introversion or extroversion.

I had my first experience with loneliness at seven years of age, when I went to a Catholic boarding school. It wasn't long before I missed my family and became incredibly homesick. To make matters worse, I felt that I didn't fit in at my new school. While I was surrounded by nuns and students who were very caring, I experienced a feeling of profound isolation.

In the beginning, it seemed as if nothing could go right for me. I vividly recall being a complete klutz in tennis and not being able to hit the ball in rounders—a game as common in Canada as baseball is in the United States or cricket is in Australia or the United Kingdom. In ballet lessons, when the instructor asked us to extend our left foot, I put out my right. I was clumsy in that too. It was more of the same in my piano lessons. I recall the piano instructor going crazy when I didn't get the notes right.

All of these acquired skills were designed to make me the perfect catch for some man one day—the ideal wife, the classic lady. I didn't quite understand what was going on as a young girl, but I knew something wasn't right for me. I was unaware that the word for what I was experiencing was *loneliness*.

In addition to being physically awkward, I excelled academically, which again left me feeling lonely and isolated from my peers for being too intelligent. I was shunned not only because I was uncoordinated, but also because I was smart.

On Fridays, we had to write a letter to our parents, which was prewritten on the chalkboard. All we had to do was copy it and fill in the blanks. I didn't do it the right way, however, because I couldn't see the use of writing a letter that someone else had constructed for me.

Then there was a party for which each of us had to dress in a specific costume. My mother, who was then attending university abroad to obtain her degree, sent me the ballerina costume that I wanted, but I felt awful wearing the costume because the skirt was too long. Later in life, I mentioned it to my mother, who was horrified because, as it turns out, she had asked the nuns to cut the skirt to fit me. This was never done, so I looked like a bedraggled ballerina. I had asked to be a dancer, even though it was something I knew I was never meant to be, because I wanted to fit in.

I also felt lonely because of my shoes. We had three outfits: one for school in the daytime, one for the afternoon, and one for Sundays, when we wore our saddle shoes and bobby socks, gray skirts, and pink blouses. Most of the boarders wore brown penny loafers with their afternoon uniforms, but not me. Mom had bought me a brown pair of Clarks shoes with crepe soles. Sundays were fine, but Mondays through Saturdays were a problem. Those Clarks were the ugliest things God ever created, in my opinion! But I wore them, and I was ridiculed for it. I remember going to Mother Anne Marie and saying, "Can you please get me a pair of penny loafers?" and her replying that she didn't think she could.

That feeling of not fitting in was my first experience of loneliness.

Because of these incidents and the impact they had on me, I became interested in loneliness at a very young age. Even though I was surrounded by people who cared for me, I still felt lonely and disconnected. When I was young, I couldn't put into words what was wrong and didn't know how to express my feelings to my parents. So, I would write them ghastly letters lying about how wonderful it was in boarding school to assuage their anxiety.

The purpose of my story is to emphasize that there are days when we all wake up and think:

"I don't fit in."

"I don't think anyone truly knows me."

"I just don't feel like I have a friend that I can call for help right now."

Sometimes we all need to be reminded that these feelings are entirely normal. What's *not* normal, however, are prolonged periods of disconnection that lead to emotional suffering. After all, the existence of durable, intimate social and emotional bonds is a crucial component in living a happy life. We need to be able to confide in others, be accepted for who we are, and genuinely feel as if we belong. We also want to receive and provide support. It's critical that we feel *a part of* and not *apart from* whatever we do in life.

Over a lifetime, people can experience different levels of loneliness and social isolation, depending on their personal situations at any particular time. Two individuals could be in the same situation and be surrounded by the same group of people but have altogether different experiences. It depends on their specific needs for closeness and connection with others. One person may feel as if their emotional and social needs are being met while the other does not. Therefore, many different contributing factors go into determining outcomes, including expectations.

There isn't one set of rules that can apply to everyone, and currently there aren't many methods for diagnosing, preventing, and treating loneliness. Detecting loneliness isn't as easy as going into the doctor's office for an X-ray or a blood test. It's much more difficult because it encompasses many measurable and immeasurable factors that must each be carefully evaluated. Typically, medical professionals utilize a wide range of information and data to determine whether or not someone is lonely. They can look at aspects of people's lives, such as work status, size of household, current social networks, and relationship history for hard data—but this investigation also has to be taken into areas that are more difficult to quantify with numbers, such as someone's satisfaction with their relationships and their perception of the emotional support system around them.

We can also think of loneliness as a state of disharmony within multiple spheres.

Loneliness occurs when there's a disruption in one or more of the spheres. For example, there may be disharmony between the biosphere/me sphere and the social sphere that causes a domino effect that impinges on all other areas. This can lead to a loss of connection within several spheres.

For a minute, let's look at the impact one type of disruption can have on multiple spheres. People tend to get irritable at certain points in the lunar cycle. When there is greater gravitational pull between the moon and the earth, as happens during full moons, many psychiatrists report that the number of agitated people increases. Something similar happens when the sun's gravitational pull counteracts that of the moon, resulting in neap tides. During these weaker tides, emotions frequently run a little hyper or manic. It's fair to say, then, that fluctuations in moon's gravitational pull have an effect on the biosphere/me sphere, and if individual emotions are indeed running high, the lunar cycle likely has an effect on the social sphere too.

Now let's look at what happens to the terrasphere at another point in the lunar cycle. Studies suggest that water pollution, including harmful plastic, chemical waste, and bacteria, is most evident seven days following a new or full moon when tides are at their overall lowest. This point in the lunar cycle doesn't cause the damage; it simply reveals it. And the more we see the damage to the terrasphere, the more the biosphere/

The Four Spheres of Potential Disharmony

The **Biosphere/Me Sphere** refers to the individual, the body, the self, and the ego.

The **Social Sphere** refers to the relationship between the individual and the various social groups he or she interacts with. This includes altruistic acts, benevolence, and superego functions.

The **Terrasphere** refers to Earth and how the Biosphere interacts with it.

The **Theo Sphere** refers to what is beyond superego functions—i.e., spirituality or engagement in the service of a higher being. This includes the relationship between the individual and their spiritual response, and the relationship between the individual and the environment.

---

me sphere and social sphere suffer. A level of eco-anxiety has developed in recent years among people who feel that, collectively, we're not doing enough to save the planet. Those who take personal measures to recycle and reduce their carbon footprint often feel alone in this effort because individual action is simply not enough. A broader, more unified global response is needed.

On an economic level, if the funds to restore ecological balance are concentrated in the hands of one country or a small number of people within that country, a very unstable situation exists in the global social and terraspheres. The inequities will certainly be felt and seen in how effectively each country or group of people is able to enact change where they live with the resources they have. Furthermore, success in saving our planet can only be achieved if everyone is able to maximize efforts. Now you see how disruption works across the several different spheres to create a sense of disharmony and disconnection.

A similar disruption in the spheres that leads to isolation and loneliness can be seen in the proliferation of guns in the United States. I would certainly categorize the rise in gun violence as disruptions in the biosphere/me sphere and the social sphere. So, what causes people to act so violently? One cause is the "copycat" phenomenon. Kids see other kids—as they did initially in the Columbine High School massacre—shooting up their schools and gaining notoriety. But why is it that no other country has the sort of high school gun violence the United States has? It's not only how readily available guns are but also the culture that has been formed from habits and from previous experience. In a disproportionate number of school shootings, the shooters have disruption in their homes and/or feel isolated from their peers because of bullying. Larry Siegel and Chris McCormick point out that violence among youth is learned through association with deviant role models, including family members and peers.[4] The media may have an impact on a person's tendency toward violent behavior, as may certain mental disorders. There is also a strong correlation between substance abuse and violence.

By contrast, what makes a *harmonious* social sphere? I think it's a good relationship between mankind and man, and man and a supreme being, whether one calls that God or simply a higher entity outside of oneself. The result is harmony—a sense of moral values, ethics, rules, and regulation.

Harmful to Our Health

When we take a hard look at the recent compelling statistics on loneliness, we find that it's no surprise that influential people in the medical community are speaking out. Former US Surgeon General Dr. Vivek H. Murthy frequently mentions the existence of a "loneliness epidemic" in America, and has also stated that during his years caring for patients, the most common pathology he encountered wasn't heart disease or diabetes but loneliness. Take a minute to let that really sink in.

So, as you can see, feeling lonely and socially isolated have been found to make us mentally and physically ill. When we aren't being nurtured by and receiving support from others, the impact on us can be very severe. Persistent feelings of isolation have been found to have about the same effect on the human body as being overweight or smoking fifteen cigarettes a day.[5] People experiencing thoughts of loneliness are also more likely to suffer from depression, insomnia, and drug abuse. Recent statistics have shown that during a sixteen-year-period between 2001 and 2017, the total suicide rate in America increased by 31 percent.[6]

In many ways, the health hazards caused by loneliness can all be traced back to an increase of one underlying factor in our lives: stress.

Scientists say the feeling of being lonely is an evolutionary phenomenon, not unlike hunger. In the same way being hungry motivates us to find food, loneliness is supposed to prompt us to seek safety in the protection of a group setting through the body's release of stress hormones, such as cortisol. These hormones stimulate parts of the brain to make us more alert in

Major Effects of Loneliness

We see clear signs of loneliness all around us, including:

—Obesity

—Disconnection

—Depression

—Anxiety

—Stress

—Identity issues

—Interpersonal difficulties

—Suicide

—Negative addictions (such as opioid addiction)

—Risk of heart attack

—Risk of stroke

—Increased levels of stress hormones and
  inflammation

—Type 2 diabetes

—Dementia

dangerous situations. While this is essential in a fight-or-flight crisis, prolonged exposure to stress hormones can do plenty of damage to our health. Feeling lonely can also exacerbate symptoms of existing mental health disorders and contribute to the development of additional psychological issues. It can also make it even more difficult for people to reach out and ask for help.

In any case, loneliness is, without a doubt, one of the most potent obstacles to health and happiness. But why has this feeling been occurring in such record numbers of people in modern times? Let's take a look at some factors that have contributed to our loneliness over the last few decades.

Changing Households

The most recent US census data shows that more than a quarter of the population lives alone—the highest rate ever recorded. According to other research, the average American's number of close confidants decreased by more than 30 percent between 1985 and 2009. The aging of the Baby Boomer generation (those born between 1946 and 1964) is one reason for this. Approximately one out of every eleven Baby Boomers doesn't have a romantic partner, spouse, or living child, and one in six lives by themselves. Overall, Boomers have had fewer children than their parents did, and more divorces. Because of these factors, many don't have anyone to grow old with.

Today, over 45 percent of the adult population in America is single, which is more than ever before in the history of the country.[7] If we compare that percentage to the fact that 72 percent of the adult population was married in 1960, we can see how much our households have transformed over the decades. It's also crucial to note that those who choose to get married and have children today are doing so much later in life, so the median age of first marriages is higher than it has ever been. This delay in establishing families is undoubtedly another contributor to feelings of isolation and loneliness, as people experience loneliness in the years leading up to marriage, and given women's ages when they do get married, they elect to have fewer children.

Aging Population

Loneliness among the elderly is marked by feelings of isolation, lack of companionship, and an inability to perform daily activities such as self-care and meal preparation.

Antonella was born in Italy and relocated to Canada when she was seventeen years old. Today she's in her seventies, and after suffering a terrible accident, she reports that she has no one she can turn to for help. She feels shame and embarrassment that her adult children aren't there for her; they're preoccupied with their own lives and often say they'll come and visit, but never do. Moreover, Antonella raised her daughter's son as her own, and even he refuses to help her do the chores around the house that she can no longer perform on her own.

She was especially disappointed when she looked at her neighbors in Edmonton's large Ukrainian community, where it's customary for all generations to lend one another a hand. There, the community is more important than the individual. Antonella felt demoralized because her adult children weren't helping her the way many of the adult children in the Ukrainian families around her helped their elders. Over time, she became frustrated and short-tempered. She resented the fact that she was physically unable to do the things she used to be able to do, and that she was seeing a side of her children that she hadn't noticed before.

"I can't believe they're like this," she said tearfully.

In therapy, she learned to make gentle but clear and firm requests, and to move from anger to developing realistic expectations of her daughters. More important, she was able to be assertive with her grandson. In the past, she would guilt him and her grown children, labeling them selfish. Gradually, she was able to discover where the underlying anger came from—namely, hurt from her expectations not being met. Her marriage wasn't fulfilling, either; her husband was ten years older than she was and believed in traditional roles, so he left her to do most of the work around the home. In therapy she came to understand and accept that while she couldn't change him, she could change herself so that she could look at the situation and not feel hurt. "I see the mess in the living room, and now I realize it means I have a husband."

Eventually, Antonella's children came around and gave her what she needed, which was not simply physical help but also emotional support. She longed to feel that she was needed and important in their lives. Her children were invited in for a few sessions with Antonella and her husband and together they were able to work through some of these unresolved conflicts and to live in a more harmonious, less painful way. Due primarily to financial constraints, they were unable to provide their mother with a caregiver or domestic help, but they worked it out among themselves and with their husbands so that they were able to give her some support. Prior to this, Antonella had felt like a victim. She felt that the more she gave, the more her children expected from her. She also felt that they should give her something in return since she was sick, yet nothing was forthcoming. Once she realized what she needed and set about getting it in a less aggressive way, her mood changed, and there was a resurfacing of a softness in her eyes and a gentleness in her demeanor that had always been there before the accident. She still felt that she should be able to bake and to carry on with other traditional Italian customs, but she also realized that was not going to be in the cards for her now. She accepted that she had undergone some physical changes that would preclude her from participating in these activities, and she resolved to work around them. Occasionally, she was able to invite her daughters to come for a morning to bake, sing, and play music together, which was uplifting for everyone.

Changing Workplace

One of the primary locations where our sense of loneliness can increase or decrease is in the workplace, since we spend a considerable amount of our time there. One study found that we are "almost as likely to have daily contact with our colleagues as we are with our children."[8]

Workplace loneliness has been and continues to be a vital subject of discussion in the corporate world. We've seen the way feelings of loneliness can affect the body, and businesses are now recognizing that they can have drastic effects on the productivity of their workforce as well.

A combination of advances in technology, the ability to work remotely, increased self-employment, and fewer human interactions has had a significant impact on loneliness levels in recent years. Due to the nature of freelance opportunities and the flexibility to select one's own work hours, it's easy for workers to lose their sense of belonging. Traditional workplaces provided people with the feeling that they were part of something larger than themselves, but these alternative work styles limit our face-to-face interactions with coworkers, which can have a lasting effect on our feelings of connectedness and can be detrimental to our happiness with our jobs and careers.

Loneliness can impair our decision making, limit our creativity, and have a severe effect on our overall productivity: the lonelier workers become, the more their job performance suffers.[9] Disconnected employees are also less approachable to colleagues and less committed to their companies. And isolation doesn't affect only individuals: through behavioral mimicry, loneliness can rapidly spread like a cold through a workspace, or any space, for that matter. This is likely the primary reason that employers began to take notice. It's also why many freelancers were increasingly gravitating toward coworking spaces before COVID-19 struck.

It's also important to note that in years past, people worked for the same company alongside the same colleagues throughout their careers until they reached the age of retirement. The workplace helped lasting friendships and even romantic relationships to flourish. But today it's increasingly difficult to establish such meaningful relationships and experience their benefits in the work environment, as the typical employee remains at a company for an average of fewer than two years. Although we want to feel that we're connecting with our coworkers and contributing to the greater good through our jobs, the numbers show that this is not the experience most of us are having. Approximately how prevalent is loneliness at work? One study found that around 42 percent of people don't have a coworker they would consider a friend.[10]

For decades, workers have been able to pursue any dream and become whatever they want to be. It's been quite common for people to leave their hometowns and families behind to pursue larger salaries in different locations. The widespread availability of opportunity has proved to be a significant blessing for many in terms of their careers, but it's also something of a curse when it comes to people's personal lives. It's challenging to maintain meaningful relationships as people move from job to job and city to city, or as steady work becomes harder to find.

Even though it's been discovered that working longer hours leads employees to ignore interpersonal relationships, we seem to be putting in more and more time on the job.[11] It appears that working to excess has become the standard over the last few decades. We've almost arrived at a point where working forty hours a week is seen by many as not working enough!

In the future, changes in the workplace and how we choose to work will only make those meaningful relationships even more challenging to establish and continue. It will be interesting to see how the issue of loneliness is addressed as we adapt, evolve, and reconfigure our work environments in a much-anticipated post-pandemic era, and in the various interim stages.

Changing Technology

On the surface, I think we would all agree that in a technical sense, communication these days couldn't be easier. Unlimited access to family, friends, coworkers, and, well, *anyone* is right at our fingertips. Reaching out and interacting is only a quick swipe, a tap, or a few keystrokes away. We can virtually order any product or meal or even a ride to go on a date, all from the comfort of our own homes. At the same time, emerging technologies such as video calling, livestreaming, and any of the dozens of available social media platforms allow us to be digitally linked to hundreds, thousands, or even *millions* of "followers," "friends," and "connections."

And yet, despite all of these possible options, people of all ages and backgrounds have found it incredibly challenging to connect. They've been talking *at* one another instead of *with* one another. And, worse, some have stopped talking at all! Teenagers communicate primarily through text messages. They participate in group texts, yet never speak to one another directly. I've had patients who mostly communicate with their children via a device, even when they're all under the same roof! And don't forget the family that dines together but never looks up from their phones, let alone engages in any dialogue.

Typed messages have taken the place of face-to-face encounters and interactions. One study reported that approximately 30 percent of Americans are unable to sit through an entire meal without checking their phones.[12]

The more advanced we've become technologically, the more divorced we've become emotionally. A crucial component of establishing meaningful relationships with others is the exchange of emotion. Although text messages and e-mails have brought convenience, they've also stripped away much of the personality. Think of it as *communicating without connecting*. We don't need to have face-to-face conversations all the time, but more recently we've begun to realize how essential those human interactions are to feeling genuinely connected. If there was a silver lining in being forced to remain at home in order to flatten the curve of a deadly virus, it was that we resumed some form of connected dialogues. Being with our families twenty-four seven and communicating via Zoom or FaceTime calls with distanced friends and colleagues have made us look at one another again when we communicate.

Changing Religion

Traditionally, places of worship have served as centers for social and cultural life. A person's faith helped them to navigate the inevitable ups and downs of existence, and overall, participation in religion typically made people healthier and happier. The spiritual landscape has changed drastically in the past few decades, however; by and large, we're gradually drifting away from organized religion. Participation in faith groups, which have historically served as the most significant belief-based communities, is also in steep decline. The percentage of Americans who report belonging to a synagogue, church, or mosque is at an all-time low, averaging 50 percent.[13] The percentage of Americans with no religious affiliation at all—also known as the *nones*—has doubled since 2000, making *no religion* the fastest growing religion in the country.

Changing Politics

Is America's increasingly polarized political climate also contributing to our nation's sense of loneliness? It seems very likely when you look at the current state of local and national government and what's happening with political parties. And I believe this works both ways—that perhaps some of the viciousness found on social media and other outlets can be attributed to our deep feelings of isolation. Loneliness makes people much less empathetic and more likely to see the world in a very polarized way. When we don't feel connected to others, it's easy for us to adopt a detached "them versus us" outlook on politics and life.

If we're not interacting, discussing, and debating ideas, we can become distanced and less open to accepting differing thoughts and viewpoints. This makes us even more mentally and physically closed off from the outside world. It seems that in response to losing their sense of connection with those around them, more and more people are resorting to political tribalism to find community. It seems that exchanges of ideas and opposing thoughts in face-to-face meetings have all but disappeared—or, worse, are surfacing in negative ways, such as shouting at others over social media. This is yet another contributing factor to our widening feelings of not belonging.

Changing Communities

The statistics on loneliness are an indication that there is also a social disintegration taking place in our communities. If individuals are struggling, then there's an excellent chance that cities and towns are too. One in five Americans say they aren't satisfied with the quality of life in their communities and are frequently lonely (Pew Research Center, 2018).[14] The only way we've been able to get to a place of such personal loneliness is through a breakdown in the many forms of community we inhabit. Logically, individuals and community have a symbiotic relationship. One can't thrive without the success of the other. In the same way that feeling disconnected from family members in the home or colleagues in the workplace causes a sense of loneliness, not being able to connect with neighbors generates a tremendous sense of isolation. In contrast, when a person feels a solid sense of community, their levels of satisfaction and happiness are positively impacted.

In his book *The Vanishing Neighbor: The Transformation of American Community*, author Marc J. Dunkelman says that over the past few decades, we've lost touch with our community-based roots. Instead of participating in our local environments, we take part in new social networks in which we maintain connections only with our closest family and friends. He further explains that each of us has three rings of personal relationships shaping our social communities:

The Inner Ring: close family and personal friends
The Middle Ring: members of the "township" or neighborhood
The Outer Ring: people who are impersonal or unfamiliar (e.g., distant Facebook friends, and so forth.)

Dunkelman says that the middle rings that have always brought people together in local communities are disappearing. Our experience of in-person interactions with those around us, especially our neighbors, has also dwindled. He goes on to state that "the sorts of relationships my grandparents had taken for granted while raising their children—between neighbors and colleagues, often across generations—had withered, and others had begun to take their place. Over the course of several decades, the nation's social architecture had been upended."[15]

Decades ago, the meaning of community was very different from what it is today. People were more likely to know those who delivered packages to their homes, for example, and neighbors were seen as extensions of the family and supported one another in the raising of one another's children. Many worked together in local shops and other businesses. Theirs was not a village of gossip but instead a place where people helped and supported one another. Today, however, it appears that our connections with the environment around us are fading. There are too many people who feel that they don't have a place to call home or a community where they truly feel they belong.

At one time, the local community was an essential place in people's lives because it was where nearly everything occurred. We lived with our families, went to school with our close friends, and encountered danger and overcame adversity together. It was also where we witnessed local role models achieve greatness and move on to bigger and brighter endeavors. For a variety of reasons, we just play with our digital devices when gathered with our families. We text with our friends or post to one another's social media pages and watch video clips of people all over the world without ever coming into contact with other human beings.

Yet it is in this loneliness that the deepest activities begin. It is here that you discover act without motion, labor that is profound repose, vision in obscurity, and, beyond all desire, a fulfillment whose limits extend to infinity.
— Thomas Merton

The experience of loneliness should not only be a clear indication to us that our emotional and physical needs are not being met, but it should also serve as a critical motivator for us to change our behavior. It should be an immediate signal to connect with others, especially if we're in a transitional period, such as moving to a new city, going through a challenging time, or beginning a new job. What it shouldn't be is a chronic condition in which we decide we're lonely and then become withdrawn, introverted, and less approachable to others for extended periods of time. Once loneliness becomes an established sentiment in our lives, it's easy for us to remain this way, and it develops into a cycle that's more and more difficult to break. It can even lead to destructive behaviors and addictions that contribute to the overall problem.

How you respond to loneliness is a choice, one that you have total control over. It's a hard habit to break but critical to overcome as you march toward happiness. It's easy to say, "Just get out of the house" or, "Call your family or friends" when you feel despair. The hard work is *doing* it. If you allow yourself to stay lonely and isolated, the impact can be downright dangerous. As the saying goes, "It's not how hard you fall, it's how quickly you get back up." The Harvard Study of Adult Development, which started in 1937 and is now being directed by psychiatrist Robert Waldinger, is a longitudinal study that attempts to predict the factors that contribute to happiness by tracking the health of over 775 men over the age of eighty. What do you think the study found? It was not middle-aged cholesterol levels that predicted how happy the study participants would be when they grew old but how satisfied they were in their relationships with family, friends, and marriages.[16]

chapter four

··

NEGATIVE ADDICTIONS

We first make our habits, and then our habits make us.
—John Dryden

Prolonged periods of loneliness, isolation, and depression bring on immense emotional pain. As much as we sometimes desperately try to avoid admitting that we feel this way, we eventually have to decide how we're going to address the problem. Loneliness impacts our brains in such a way that causes us to have less control over our behaviors, emotions, and cravings. So, without a social network in place to provide us with understanding and emotional support, we're more likely to seek out dangerous habits and harmful addictions, especially in the form of substance abuse. We do so hoping that these habits will provide emergency—albeit temporary—relief of our symptoms.

Although they can be incredibly damaging to our health and happiness, addictions often seem to be the easiest remedies a person can turn to for help in taking away their emotional pain and discomfort. When these dependences result in unfavorable circumstances, the addictions can be defined as negative. And it can happen to anyone! Reliance on a substance such as alcohol or a behavior such as gambling can take over a life, no matter how grand or humble that life seems. We engage in self-soothing actions for a quick fix, a mental and physical distraction of sorts to reduce our distress—and although these actions can prove successful in the short term, they can become learned, unconscious, and permanent habits over time. In effect, once our discomfort subsides, we're stuck with them.

Loneliness and addiction feed off each other and can establish collective momentum if either isn't adequately addressed. In abusing dangerous substances or engaging in harmful behaviors to alleviate their painful emotions, people often shut out friends and family to concentrate on their relationship with these addictions, alienating those around them. So, by seeking a quick relief for their feelings of loneliness, they end up worsening the situation.

The next logical question is, "In addition to unhappiness and loneliness, what else leads us to turn to negative addictions?"

Addiction often involves cycles of relapse and remission. Most of us recognize this, whether our dependence is on caffeine, sugar, or amphetamines. We'll swear to stop, even enlist support, halt for a time, and then experience recidivism. "I don't have an addiction," we say. Well, denial is a sure sign of one!

Though substance abuse is what we usually think of when the topic of negative addiction comes up, there are many other forms, such as cell phone use, Internet surfing, watching videos

Contributors to Negative Addictions

In addition to loneliness and isolation, some common factors leading to negative addiction include:

—Being in the constant presence of an addict.
—Being on prescription medications that have the potential to be addictive.
—Having physical or mental health problems.
—Being from or in a family with a history of addiction.
—Being in a high-stress vocation or life situation.

online, gaming, social networking, gambling, and others. Additionally, there are often-overlooked or misunderstood areas of emotional and sexual addictions.

Not feeling is no replacement for reality. Your problems today are still your problems tomorrow.
~ Larry Michael Dredla

Real estate coach and business entrepreneur Tom Ferry has come up with four addictions that he insists "destroy more dreams, hopes, and lives than drugs, alcohol, food, gambling, or sex combined." Ferry believes these typical vices are actually byproducts or effects brought on by four much larger causes that are the real roots of the problem.

Four Dangerous Addictions

ADDICTION TO THE OPINIONS OF OTHER PEOPLE

As a society, we're addicted to what others think about us and how others' views of the world affect us.

Over the past thirty-five years, I've encountered many patients who are so obsessed with what other people think that they've forgotten who they are. One case in point was Mary, whose overriding concern for the opinions of others kept her in a bad marriage. She believed that if she left, people would judge her poorly and consider her a failure. The marriage was abusive: her husband routinely beat her in a drunken stupor, and in his more sober states mentally and verbally abused her by criticizing everything she did or didn't do. To complicate the relationship even more, they had three children together. The irony was that she lived in a rural community where everyone knew everyone else's business, so surely people had already formed ideas about her. Still, Mary kept her troubles to herself and tried harder and harder to cope. I felt a chill as she expressed the horror of this relationship that spanned decades. She had forgotten who she was. At one time in her life, she played the piano, but no longer did so. She used to like reading; now, she had no time for such an activity. She used to take good care of her physical appearance; now she was disheveled and unkempt. The bottom line was that she refused to get out of a damaging marriage for fear of what the people around her would think.

The story of Peter, an entrepreneur, also comes to mind. He was married to a successful attorney, and the harder he tried to please her, the more she demeaned him. He stayed in the

relationship because of their children and because of his need-
iness. He relied on his wife to feel good about himself. Over
time, she became an object of success for him. She was very
beautiful and had a well-appointed wardrobe. Peter construed
that being with her meant he was successful as well.

It took a long time in therapy to determine exactly what
he wanted and needed in his life. Did he need to be routinely
castigated for not producing the income that his wife felt he
should? Did he need to be reprimanded like a child because a
business deal had fallen through? Did he need to consistently
be rejected sexually?

Eventually, they both attended a session together. I recall
his wife being extremely angry at him. She appeared very well
put together, with her Gucci shoes, Louis Vuitton handbag, and
Armani suit. From her perspective, she had already cheated
on him and couldn't understand why he would remain with
her when she didn't really care whether he stayed or left. She
pointed out that she'd tried very hard to get him to leave, and
that his reluctance to do so made her lose respect for him. He
was crushed when she spoke in such a derogatory way about
him. He begged her for yet another chance.

Peter's was an interesting case, because he had to work
through some childhood issues involving dependency and
parental injunctions. In his mind, he worried, "What would
the neighbors say? What would people think?" He was raised
in a strict Catholic home in which divorce was not acceptable.
A recurring refrain was, "As you make your bed, you lay in it."
He felt that if only he could do a little bit more, his wife would
appreciate him. He kept pretending that he had the perfect
marriage—the son, the daughter, the wife, the membership at a

prestigious golf club, and so on. He lived in an exclusive area of the city. But then he started peeling the layers of the onion. One day he said, amid a lot of tears, "Who am I in all of this? Why am I doing this? What is this all about?" This was an epiphany for him, to suddenly realize that what he had been doing with his life wasn't really what he needed to do but what he assumed other people felt that he should do. "I don't know how to start dating," he confided. He didn't know how to march to the beat of his own drum. Eventually, though, he moved out and moved on.

ADDICTION TO DRAMA

Some people are drawn to and consumed by any event or situation that occupies their thoughts and fills their mind with negativity, which often brings attention to them in unproductive ways.

I'm sure you've all heard the expression, "Oh, there goes a drama queen." Samantha was an extremely attractive thirty-five-year-old woman. She was married to a dentist and had three active young boys, ages ten, eight, and six. She was so concerned about her appearance and having gained some weight over the holiday season that she was unable to look at anything in her life in a positive way. She construed that her husband didn't appreciate her as much as he used to, and, more important, that he wasn't sexually attracted to her. Then she discovered by going through his computer that he was looking at pornography. She confronted him with her findings and became so consumed with his egregious act that she was unable to see anything good in her life.

Samantha decompensated rapidly and started thinking that she needed to leave the marriage, that her husband didn't love her, that the children were a burden, and that she was losing her mind. She wept often as she dwelled on her husband's interest in erotica and other things that were negative in her life, all of which she believed had been triggered by her weight gain. After the pornography episode, she and her husband slept in different rooms for months. Every time her husband tried to get close to her, she pushed him away. "How can I forgive him?" she asked me.

When I asked her if he had ever viewed pornography before, she was adamant that this was the first time and it was all her fault. She doubled back and asked her husband that same question, to which he responded, "Yes, several times." After seeing how hurt she was, he promised he wouldn't do it again. So here she was, addicted to looking at the negatives in her life, and there he was, "addicted" to pornography. She had a moral dilemma: Was it okay for her husband to view pornography or not, and what did it say about their marriage? There were hurt and betrayal, followed by growth and self discovery. I asked her whether she was ready to develop a new marriage—a second marriage—with Joe, her husband.

There was an additional area in which Samantha was addicted to drama. She had a very close girlfriend with whom she'd had a falling out, apparently because the girlfriend said that she was taking a break from their friendship to spend time with other friends in her life. Samantha felt that the lives of her children and of her friend's children were intertwined since they were engaged in many of the same extracurricular activities. She responded to her friend's wish to engage with other friends as a complete rejection. This all-or-nothing thinking meant, from Samantha's perspective, that something was wrong with her. It took quite a long time for her to see the situation differently and to realize that perhaps it was a healthy thing to branch out and form other friendships, and to understand that her friend's decision to go a separate way wasn't necessarily a rejection of Samantha but rather an opportunity for growth.

It was interesting to see how that addiction to drama played out not only in her marriage but also in her relationships with other people. Next, Samantha started questioning her effectiveness as a parent because her sons seemed to obey her husband, yet displayed oppositional, defiant behavior with her. Over time, she was able to work through her parenting issues and realize that instead of taking it all so personally, she needed to distance herself from it. Samantha learned to ask herself, "What kinds of things am I doing to cause this? What kinds of things is my husband doing to bring about a different outcome? What is my takeaway?"

ADDICTION TO THE PAST

People with this particular fixation have an unhealthy attachment to events or situations that have occurred in the past. They're stuck in how things used to be.

Eleanor's mother told her that she would never amount to anything. Even though she'd become a family physician of some prominence, Eleanor kept remembering what her mother had always said. She was still convinced that she was useless on many levels. No matter how well she did as a doctor, she felt as though she were just an imposter.

"Am I doing a good job, or did I con them? Did I do well in med school, or did they just think I was good?" she asked. Then she added, "Because my mother told me I wasn't good enough, and that I would amount to nothing."

"What about your dad?" I asked.

"My dad was ineffectual. My mother ran the home."

As she grew up, Eleanor entered into a few relationships in which she was rejected, and again she blamed herself. The words of her mother continued to echo in her mind: she wasn't good for anything.

Fortunately, once Eleanor was able to work through her self-esteem issues—a process that was painful and difficult at times—she was able to leave the past where it belonged and move forward to develop healthy relationships. More important, she was able to say with a measure of pride, "You know, Joan, I'm a good doctor, and I'm a good person. I'm growing to like myself." Ultimately, Eleanor was able to free herself from the past.

Then there's the case of Mark, who went to work one day and was told that he had to leave his job because the company was downsizing. He took it personally, and decided that the loss of his position had to do with him and not with an economic downturn. When Mark came to see me, he was convinced that being let go was all his fault. He proceeded to tell me that there were several job interviews he had gone to where he was rejected. He was convinced that there was something wrong with him.

A change for the better started when Mark began examining what was right for him in terms of a job. What did he really want to do? And to what extent was the past affecting his present? Was he perhaps presenting himself as a failure in the interviews? We had an interesting session in which we filmed him so he could see the way he conducted himself during interviews. It was instantly clear why people rejected him: he hadn't realized it until we watched the interview together, but he was putting himself down. Seeing it for himself was enough to help turn things around.

When Anna was nineteen, she was rejected by a boyfriend, convincing her that she would never be loved. Over the ensuing years, she entered into relationships that were self-destructive and that ended badly, causing her a lot of pain. She construed that it was all her fault because her first boyfriend had dumped her. She believed that this was going to be her lot in life; she hadn't realized that it was her half-hearted efforts to meet new people that kept her from experiencing healthy relationships. It was almost as if Anna were constantly running a movie in her mind about the way things happened the night she was dumped by that initial boyfriend. She was unable to move past that event to see the productive things in her life. Eventually, she made strides and was able to put the trauma of that breakup into perspective. From there, she started being clear with herself about what it was she was looking for and focusing on some of the things she wanted and needed in a relationship. When last I heard from her, she was involved with a new man who was very different from the men she had previously dated.

ADDICTION TO WORRY

This addiction comprises all the negative and self-defeating thoughts that make us anxious, disturbed, upset, and stressed—all the thoughts that hold us back in life.[1]

Worrywarts—we all know people like that, right? They tend to look at life through a very pessimistic lens. No matter how good things are, they manage to find a way to worry about what isn't there instead of appreciating what is.

This brings to mind Greg, a forty-year-old man who was married to a university professor. Greg had moved from Ontario, leaving his position at a real estate firm where he was a top broker so his wife could take a tenured position in Alberta. After the move, he worried that he wouldn't be as successful as he was in the past. He would say, "You never know when the other shoe is going to drop," or "When you're at the top, there's only one place to go: down."

That, in essence, was Greg. He suffered full-blown anxiety attacks and was constantly worried about what would happen in the future. When he and his wife had tried to conceive and discovered that his sperm count was low, he berated himself for that too. It was all his fault that they adopted a child who subsequently died. He also irrationally believed that it was his fault the child had a congenital defect that caused his death. No matter where he went or what he did, Greg felt inadequate. He worried about what people would think, and about what his father would say because he'd left his successful career to come to Alberta, where he was unable to find work that made him feel productive or accomplished. When he went to campus, he recoiled from the other professors, who, he felt, looked at him as though he were a parasite, a pariah. His parents were coming from Ontario to visit him soon, and he was concerned that his father would think he had amounted to nothing. Would they say that he was useless? That his wife's income was supporting him? Or that he was a failure? Would they find fault with the bathroom renovations he'd done? These were his preoccupations.

Greg's tendency to worry began after he was left unattended by his family of origin when he was just eight years old. Not only would he worry but he would also ruminate about everything that could go wrong. I vividly recall him saying one day, "You know what, Joan? I'm going to open my own business. I'm going to do the research, pick a franchise, and just do it." He was very enthused.

The following week he appeared crushed.

"It wasn't going to work," he said. "How could it possibly work? How could I possibly think I could do that?" This expectation of failure that plagued him was solidified when, as young boy, he would show his father his report card and hear such comments as, "You brought home an A. Where's the A-plus?" Or, "You brought home a ninety. Where's the one hundred?" This fueled Greg's tendency to worry. It led him to compete with himself in a self-destructive way.

We worked on Greg's worries by focusing on his habit of looking at the glass as half empty. Over time, he started to look at things in a more realistic way. It was difficult work for him, and every so often he would regress. But, fortunately, he would catch himself and say, "That's what I used to do in the past. I'm not going to do it in the future."

To better understand the addiction to worry, it's essential to take a look at what Tony Robbins believes are the Six Human Needs that we have in common.[2] He listed these needs in an article I read in *Entrepreneur* magazine. When I read this, I thought he was right: each need is crucial, because all our behavior can be boiled down to an attempt to meet one or more of these needs. If we want to be happy and healthy, we must make every effort to satisfy the needs equally.

The Six Essential Human Needs

We all have these needs, but how many of them are you meeting?

1. **Certainty:** The assurance that you can avoid pain and gain pleasure.
2. **Uncertainty/Variety:** The need for the unknown, for change, for new stimuli.
3. **Significance:** The feeling that we are each unique, important, special, or needed.
4. **Connection/Love:** The yearning for closeness or union with someone or something.
5. **Expansion of Capacity/Capability/Understanding:** The need to learn, grow, and develop.
6. **Contribution:** The sense of service and the focus on helping, giving, and supporting others.

When everything seems to be going against you, remember that the airplane takes off against the wind, not with it.
~ Henry Ford

When your life feels out of whack because you've fallen victim to one or more of the four addictions or aren't consistently fulfilling the six basic human needs, you instinctively seek comfort, often in negative addictions. But hazardous activities only momentarily allow us to feel that we're no longer in distress. They provide a false sense of comfort that leads us to repeat the pattern to the point where we can become dependent on the substance, activity, or behavior. A harmful addiction is an uncontrollable involvement in a practice that provides immediate gratification but may be perilous in either the short or long run. In becoming addicted, a person loses at least some measure of control in his or her life. Although the continuance of the behavior has negative consequences for the individual and those around him or her, the person simply can't stop themselves from engaging in it.

Carol was going through the motions of daily life—dropping her children off at school, coming back home, preparing meals, getting involved with the community. But all the while she felt a tremendous sense of unhappiness. She didn't understand where the sadness came from, because on paper she seemed to have everything she needed. She was married to a physician and was able to stay at home to raise her three young children, who were very busy with extracurricular activities. But even though she attended school meetings and did lots of things for her children and her husband, she often felt as if she were just standing on the periphery, looking in at other people's lives from a distance. When looking at her own life, she felt a lack of joy, energy, and connection.

One of the effects she experienced as a result of this mindset was a low-grade form of depression, referred to as dysthymia. Because of this persistent depressive disorder, one of the things she became disconnected from was her body, which eventually caused her to routinely binge-eat. She felt so detached from the way she looked that she would buy dresses in three different sizes to wear depending on how much weight she had lost or regained.

Carol's loneliness facilitated her binge-eating, and her ultimate addiction to food. Hers was a very poignant case of being disconnected. The lonelier she felt, the more she binged; the more she binged, the more disconnected she felt from her body. The vicious cycle continued. Her isolation and lack of a support network were major contributing factors to her eating disorder. I believed that this negative addiction—the binge-eating— would stop once the dysthymia lifted and Carol felt reengaged in life and reconnected with others. This was a long process for her because she had never really learned to trust other people, and other women in particular. Once she was able to connect with one or two people, she felt less isolated. She'd always had artistic tendencies, so she joined a pottery class where she met other women who shared her interests and taught her new techniques, and in time she became less introverted. The negative addiction stopped. Carol's case perfectly illustrates how loneliness and isolation can be fertile grounds for the breeding of negative addictions.

You leave old habits behind by starting out with the thought, "I release the need for this in my life."
~ Wayne Dyer

For some people, food is an addiction; they eat to feel better. Others turn to substances of a different kind. Their reasons for doing so are varied. Many do it to feel better, seeking relief

Substances People Often Become Addicted To

The following are among the most common and addictive substances in our culture:

—Tobacco

—Caffeine

—Alcohol

—Strong stimulants (cocaine, methamphetamine)

—Opioid painkillers (oxycodone, codeine, heroin)

—Hallucinogens (PCP, LSD, Ayahuasca)

—Inhalants (glue, paint thinner)

—Sedatives and tranquilizers (antianxiety medications)

from stress. Some do it to feel good; they seek to experience pleasure or a high. And still others do it to increase their performance—to do better.[3] There are also other components at play here, including peer pressure and overall curiosity: we're tempted to experiment with behaviors, activities, and substances that others are already engaged in if we believe they'll provide us with one of the above results. The latest trend among those seeking a quick fix or shortcut to spiritual enlightenment is the Ayahuasca craze. Ayahuasca is a tea brewed from hallucinogenic plants found in the Amazon rainforest. Personally, I don't understand the appeal; why would anyone want to quaff a horrible-tasting beverage that first makes you violently ill and then keeps you impaired for an entire weekend? Still, people are drawn to this perceived panacea, this supposed cleanse for their psyche. Trends like this worry me because of the dangers involved and the possibly lasting effects on the body and mind. You can't wipe away negative emotion by drinking tea and hallucinating.

Emotional Addiction

So far, we've talked about being addicted to a particular substance or behavior, but is it possible to be addicted to an emotion? Of course! Ask anyone who's been in love.

Scholars Patrick Spröte and Roland W. Fleming assert that we experience adverse events, interpret them, and then create a general rule that shapes our perception.[4] We then see the world through the lens of one of three emotions: anger, fear, or sadness. In other words, we become addicted to that emotion.

Anger can appear as a fit of rage, mood swings, and/or low frustration tolerance. It can manifest in dissatisfaction, disappointment, and/or resentment.

Fear can appear as a lack of trust in yourself or others, hesitation, indecision, doubt, anxiety, and even procrastination or avoidance.

Sadness can appear as apathy, indifference, helplessness, or a sense of deficit. It is also evident in those who always see the glass as half empty.

An emotional addiction not only colors the world but can also be a crutch. It becomes a familiar framework within which to deal with life. When this happens, we can be held back, restrained and entrapped in a loop of painful feelings and reactions. It's useful to be aware of our emotional well-being, to examine our overall state of mind, and to assess our degree of harmful emotional dependency.

Earlier we covered Tom Ferry's Four Addictions, which I believe can all be subsumed under emotional addiction because they relate back to being fearful. As with any addiction, you need to take stock of yourself and find out whether you're an emotional addict. Do you usually respond to situations with anger? Fear? Sadness? Do you pause, or do you just react immediately? Are you dependent on those emotions because they seem to be your MO, your only way of being with people? If so, how does that dependence affect your relationships with yourself and with others? Most emotional addicts leave a trail of pain and suffering in their wake.

Love Addiction

In the 1970s and '80s, the concept of *love addiction* came to public attention with Stanton Peele's 1975 book *Love and Addiction*. The twelve-step program Sex and Love Addicts Anonymous (SLAA), which hosts meetings based on a philosophy similar to that of Alcoholics Anonymous, was founded in 1976, shortly after the book's publication. Sex and love addictions have been defined as intimacy disorders in which rumination or constant thoughts about the sexual act or a fantasy relationship result in barriers between the addict and others.

Love addiction symptoms include:

- Inability to stop seeing a specific person, even though that person is destructive to you.
- Getting "high" from romance, fantasy, or sexual intrigue.
- Using sexual relationships to try to deal with or escape from life's problems.

- Feeling desperation or dis-ease when away from one's sexual or romantic partner.

Criteria for sex addiction include:
- Excessive amounts of time spent obtaining sex, engaging in sexual activity, or recovering from sexual experiences.
- A need to increase the intensity, frequency, and number of sexual risk behaviors to achieve the desired effect.
- Experiencing distress, anxiety, irritable mood swings, and restlessness if unable to engage in sexual behavior.

Martin was addicted to pornography. His wife had recently found out about this and suggested that he go to therapy. Martin was a land developer, and his wife worked for his company. When he was out of the building, she assumed that he was providing business quotations for customers. Instead, he was covertly finding time to go to massage parlors and to masturbate to pornography. In therapy, he mentioned that he had used pornography since he was a teenager. Moreover, going to massage parlors, as he saw it, wasn't harmful to his marriage, since he wasn't being unfaithful to his wife. He felt driven to do this and wondered how he could stop it.

The real question was whether Martin *wanted* to stop it. He was ambivalent, and until he resolved that ambivalence, work on the addiction had to wait. I saw him a couple of months later. His appearance had changed noticeably. He looked exhausted. He said that he hadn't resolved his ambivalence, but that his wife had resolved it for him by seeking a divorce. "I would like to save my marriage. I have no problem being with my wife. But I don't want to end my addiction," Martin told me.

Therein lay the dilemma. Since there were support groups in the area where he lived, I suggested that he attend one of those groups so that he might clarify whether this was something he wanted to change or not. I mentioned that I thought it was important for his wife to attend a few of the support group meetings as well. Although Martin agreed to do so, I haven't heard from him since.

This was a case in which the addiction created a compulsion within Martin that he was unable to stop on his own. From his perspective, it wasn't a matter of exerting willpower so much as it was a matter of fulfilling a need regardless of the consequences. As with most addictions, the amount of sexual activity he needed to feel that rush of dopamine in the pleasure center of his brain continually increased.

Harry, at age thirty-eight, was addicted to sex. He routinely engaged in increasingly intense sexual activities, and would often have to pay for services rendered. He wanted to stop it because, as he said, "I don't want to be hooked on anything. I have a clean life. I'm not hooked on nicotine. I don't do drugs. I don't do alcohol, except in moderation. Why can't I stop this?"

Through the long process of Harry's recovery, he looked at his needs and various ways to substitute something more rewarding for the sexual activity. He decided to put the funds he would otherwise spend on sex toward a good cause—a charitable organization that was in need. Harry moved from focusing intently on the biosphere/me sphere—what was good for himself as an individual—to looking more widely at the social sphere—what was good for the community. Incidentally, his addiction had stopped him from entering into relationships with women, since he perceived that a partner would not likely accept this behavior. He felt shame and embarrassment. Over time, Harry slowly gave himself permission (and forgiveness) for a few lapses, and after a while he experienced a real relationship, which was the carrot at the end of the stick for him. He realized that there was nothing for him in the sexual liaisons he had previously been having. His addiction had primarily been a financial relationship with a temporary release.

A few years after his therapy ended, Harry came back to see me and mentioned that he was now happily married and expecting his first child. When asked whether he still had the urge to engage in excessive sexual activity, he said yes, but he chose not to act on it. By disengaging from that behavior, Harry felt more of a sense of personal control over his life and gained self-esteem. He was more at peace with himself because this skeleton no longer lurked in his closet.

Every worthy act is difficult. Ascent is always difficult. Descent is easy and often slippery.
– Mahatma Gandhi

Now that we've talked about the more prevalent addictions, let's look deeper into the *role* addictions play in our lives, as many are developed simply through force of habit. Negative addiction is often the byproduct of what we might consider much less dangerous behavior that's repeated, and often done so subconsciously. Do you need that shot of caffeine to get moving in the morning? Do you watch television news programs even though they make you anxious? Are you a worrier? Do

Descriptors of Addictive Behaviors
According to the *DSM-5*

Let's consider some pertinent points from the *Diagnostic and Statistical Manual of Mental Disorders*, fifth edition, commonly referred to as *DSM-5*. When reading the following list, ask yourself how many—if any—of these descriptors apply to you. Honestly considering your location on this spectrum constitutes the first step toward changing it.

Assess whether the following statements apply to you:

1. Taking a substance in larger amounts or for longer than intended.
2. Wanting to cut down or stop using, but not managing to.
3. Spending a lot of time getting, using, or recovering from use of a substance.
4. Having cravings or urges for the substance.
5. Continuing to use the substance even when it causes relationship problems.
6. Not managing to do what's required at home/work/school due to substance use.
7. Using the substance again and again even when it puts you in danger.
8. Continuing to use the substance even when you know you have a physical or psychological problem caused or worsened by it.
9. Giving up important social, occupational, or recreational activities due to substance use.

10. Development of withdrawal symptoms, which can be relieved by taking more of the substance.

The severity of a substance-use disorder (aka, addiction) according to the *DSM-5* can be evaluated as follows:
—Two or three symptoms indicate a mild substance-use disorder.
—Four or five indicate a moderate substance-use disorder.
—Six or more indicate a severe substance-use disorder.

you bite your nails? Shop online at midnight? If you answered yes to any of these questions (and there are thousands more I could have asked), then there's a good chance you're addicted. Your addiction may be minor and far from life-threatening, but it's an addiction nonetheless—something that isn't entirely within your control. Addiction is a habit that has power over you. Before we move on, stop and take stock of the addictions you have or may be developing.

It is by going down into the abyss
that we recover the treasures of life.
Where you stumble, there lies your treasure.
~ Joseph Campbell

The Neurobiology of Addictions

Research indicates that drug addiction is a disease that alters the way the brain works when the drug is present. Users are compelled to use again, as the destructive consequences to health and welfare pale in comparison to the drug's powerful draw. For instance, the habit of smoking, which is an addiction, really has no upside except the momentary sense of relief. The substance is itself harmful, and we've all seen what the result of this behavior looks like. Substance-use disorders, including addiction to nicotine, cause changes in the brain's wiring that lead to distorted behavior, thinking, and bodily functions. The intense cravings for addictive substances make it nearly impossible to stop using. As time goes by, areas of the brain that relate to learning, decision making, judgment, behavior control, and memory can be drastically altered. The intoxication, or immediate effects of a drug, can provoke changes in the brain that last long after the high itself has worn off. Of course, the longer the addiction exists, the more difficult it is for a person to experience the drug's effects, as their tolerance for it has grown. The increase in dosage to approximate the same high results in even more damage.

When our attempts to attain fulfillment in life fail, we tend to settle for comfort, meeting our needs on a small scale or in particular ways—for example, via harmful addiction. And the brain *rewards* such attempts.

Extensive research spotlights the neurobiology of addictions, or how the cells of the nervous system and brain function together to mediate behavior. In other words, current research focuses on the workings of the brain at a cellular level. This exciting new direction of inquiry can open doors to understanding how parts of the brain are activated by addiction and withdrawal, and may ultimately provide helpful ideas for the treatment of negative addictions. The more informed you are about what causes change in the brain, the better prepared you'll be to manage, limit, or stop negative addictions.

Although the brain weighs only around 3.3 pounds and makes up about 2 percent of a person's body weight, it serves as the command center for the entire nervous system. It outputs information to our muscles after receiving signals from our sensory organs. The brain is made up of approximately 86 billion message-sending neurons (also known as the "gray matter") and billions of nerve fibers called axons and dendrites (the "white matter"). These neurons pass electrical or chemical signals between themselves through trillions of structures called synapses. A low-voltage electrical current passes along the neuron, causing its terminal end to release certain chemicals called neurotransmitters into the gap (or synaptic cleft) between it and nearby neurons. The neurotransmitters accumulate along the receptive dendritic spines of another neuron's dendrites, and when a certain threshold is reached, a current is initiated. That current causes the neuron to release its neurotransmitters, which in turn causes a current in the next cell, and so on.

The nature of the message a neuron sends depends on where the chain or network of firing neurons begins and ends. After decades of research and thorough scientific experimentation, we have a good understanding of which actions and sensations cause specific neurons to fire in different areas of the brain. We also know that these neural networks are selectively receptive to various neurotransmitters, of which there are about a hundred different kinds. Thus, the presence or absence of multiple neurotransmitters across different neural systems directly affects how we act and what we feel. Sensations and actions are also governed by the number and reach of the neurons in a given system. So, too, is the ease with which an electrochemical signal can flow along a given neuron.

From the womb until early childhood, the brain generates hundreds of thousands of new neurons. For a long time, it was believed that this growth substantially declines after the first few years of life and becomes rare in adulthood, occurring in only two specific regions of the brain. We'll address what new research indicates in later paragraphs, but for now, it's enough to note that after a massive growth spurt in early childhood, the nervous system begins to refine itself. Engaged pathways become better at transmitting signals, while little-used neurons grow sluggish, wither, and eventually die. In extreme cases, such as when individuals are raised in deprivation or are born without the ability to see or hear, related parts of the brain may never develop or may be recruited to support entirely different functions; indeed, early-occuring brain trauma can be compensated for by systems that take on unexpected roles. Moreover, an experience such as learning to play an instrument or acquiring a second language can improve the brain's function in memory-related tasks, even into old age. All of this should impress upon you the adaptability of your nervous system, and the physiological import of your thoughts, actions, and habits!

It's All about the Dopamine

Knowing the why and the how of dopamine's effects on the brain allows you to better understand the mechanism of addiction. The promise of bigger and better rewards can overtake our rational minds. Substances such as addictive drugs act directly on the brain's reward circuits by stimulating massive releases of dopamine, preventing its reabsorption or increasing the dendritic branching of receptive neurons. The ensuing rush reinforces the preceding behavior to an illogical extent, and competing signals attempting to stop this behavior go unheeded.

Dopamine is the primary chemical signal used in the mesolimbic system, a neural circuit that regulates movement, pleasure, and motivation. The mesolimbic system also entails communication with the prefrontal cortex, which governs executive functions such as attention, impulse control, working memory, and task-switching. Taken together, the substructures of this "reward circuit" allow us to direct our attention and energy toward pleasurable experiences—and in ordinary circumstances, that's helpful. For example, because food and drink lead to the release of dopamine, they make us "feel good," which reinforces the actions of eating and drinking and ensures our survival. Dopamine is necessary for us to experience not only the pleasure of rewarding activity but also motivation toward a reward in the first place.

Neuroplasticity to the Rescue

Traumatic experiences or harmful negative addictions can form deeply ingrained neural pathways in our brains, which grow stronger every time we abuse a substance, revisit a painful emotion, or reengage in a dangerous activity. Traditional science used to tell us that our brains eventually stopped growing and developing, so once a bad habit formed or a traumatic experience occurred, it would affect our minds in the same way forever. Because of this, we would never be able to heal completely.

Well, I've got some very good news: recent research informs us that this is not necessarily the case!

Fortunately, our brains possess an ability known as *neuroplasticity*, a term that refers to a broad set of neural processes that occur every day and give the brain the ability to continuously change throughout a person's life. This means that brain activity linked to a particular function can eventually be moved to a different location, synapses can grow stronger or weaker, and the amount of gray matter can be altered. Every message sent between two neurons can improve the fitness of that neural pathway, and such improvement becomes likelier with a higher frequency of stimulation. This process can result in small changes to single neurons, or it can affect more significant neural pathways. Neuroplasticity makes learning, memory, and habituation possible. It allows the brain to structurally and chemically reorganize itself in response to the environment.

The research on neuroplasticity tells us that the brain's neural pathways can be strengthened with repetition. You may even have heard the phrase "cells that fire together, wire together" used to describe this process. Constant repetition of an activity or behavior leads to changes in the brain's structure and in the way neurons process the experience. The bonds between neurons can also strengthen over time. Therefore, we can influence this process with our current and future thoughts and behaviors—in other words, our present and future experiences, practices, and activities can actually *rewire our minds*. Because of this, we have the ability to replace years of neglect and abuse with love and caring, allowing our brains to heal themselves over time.

So, what exactly does this mean?

Addictions are determined, but they can be defeated. Just because you've had a profoundly traumatic experience (or experiences) in the past doesn't mean you can't move in a new and positive direction in life. In the blink of an eye, you can decide to change your way of being.

One of the most damaging effects of negative addictions is that they create a barrier between you and your emotions. The addictions and behavior you engage in keep you disconnected from your feelings as long as they can fill the gigantic hole that's developed within you. So, the road out of negative addiction must include self-acceptance and getting in touch with your emotions. It also must involve learning to evaluate and assess our self-inflicted distress. Instead of running away from painful situations and feelings, we must make an effort to confront them to help continue our emotional development and healing.

But before we move into creating positive addictions, we must first look at how to reestablish our connection with ourselves.

chapter five

THE VALUE OF CONNECTION

People are like stained-glass windows. They sparkle and shine
when the sun is out, but when the darkness sets in, their true
beauty is revealed only if there is a light from within.
—ELISABETH KÜBLER-ROSS

You may be thinking, "Okay, I recognize the fact that I'm experiencing disconnection and loneliness. I also realize that I may have been engaging in self-soothing negative addictions and/or harmful behaviors. So what do I do now? How do I get back on track?"

I'm glad you asked. Now that we've covered the contributing factors of our unhappiness, the surging epidemic of loneliness, and the dangers involved in taking part in negative addictions, let's look at what we can do to assess our situation and get reconnected with our bodies and minds.

Loneliness serves as a potent reminder that for us to survive and lead happy lives, we require meaningful relationships with others. We need to be acknowledged, heard, and understood. If we experience isolation and social exclusion in our lives, we can quickly lose our sense of purpose and meaning. Loneliness is an emotion that we will suffer no matter what we try to do to prevent it. There's no reason to criticize yourself for being in this state of mind. Be kind to yourself by accepting this as fact. Don't feel guilty, ashamed, or depressed for experiencing these emotions from time to time. Permit yourself to feel lonely and isolated, but also expect yourself to do whatever it takes to move on by reconnecting within and with the world around you. Don't forget that loneliness is a feeling and not a personality trait. It's not a permanent part of you and should eventually pass.

The solution to the problem must involve evaluating and assessing our emotions and building and maintaining significant connections. To develop healthy relationships, we need to be grounded in who we are as individuals. This process includes addressing our personal needs by listening to our inner voice and doing what's necessary to achieve a better understanding of our reactions and emotions.

Just Breathe

It's much easier to detect the signals our bodies are sending when we increase their clarity by limiting or eliminating interference. Think of this process as similar to getting rid of static on a radio: you must adjust the dial to tune the signal in more clearly. It's especially challenging to quiet our minds when we feel worried or stressed. A high level of anxiety tends to override all other thoughts. Often, when we're concerned or anxious, we may not even realize it right away. Worry and anxiety, such as that brought on by loneliness and engaging in negative addictions, are future-oriented states of mind in which we're overcome by the uncertainty of what could happen. We sometimes find ourselves getting carried away by these feelings and fixating on worst-case scenarios. It's a wicked game of what-ifs.

A great way to bring yourself back to the present and center your mind is to focus on your breathing. The first thing I do in all my therapy sessions is to introduce a deep breathing exercise to help patients reach a level of calmness and comfort. After all, during a time of stress, panic, or emergency, our breathing pattern and rate can drastically change. Under these circumstances, we start breathing rapidly from our upper lungs instead of breathing slowly from our lower lungs. If this process goes on long enough without our physically exerting ourselves, we can experience painful symptoms such as confusion, dizziness, nausea, and numbness in our extremities. But the good news is that we can reverse these symptoms by paying attention to and controlling our breathing. This can lead to what's known as the body's parasympathetic response, or relaxation response. All it takes is a shift in breathing rate and pattern to make this happen.

It starts with taking deeper and slower breaths into your lower lungs. You'll notice that when you fill your lungs with air, they push down on the diaphragm, a sheetlike muscle that separates the chest from the abdomen. This causes your stomach to expand and contract with each breath. It's crucial to start with diaphragmatic breathing, which involves inhaling gradually and deeply through your nose and exhaling slowly through your mouth. The resulting calming response you've created not only decreases blood pressure and muscle tension but also instills an increased level of comfort in the body and peaceful-ness in the mind. Once we're able to remain in the present and reach that desired state, we can establish much better condi-tions for connecting with our bodies and can get in touch with where our feelings of pain and discomfort are originating in our bodies and minds.

Remember, this is a gradual process meant to open the lines of communication. We aren't climbing the entire mountain in a single day. The important thing is to get you in touch with what you're feeling and to remind yourself that with the proper effort and focus, you can control your body's responses. Now, that's an epiphany!

Alone Time

It's critical to understand that loneliness and being alone are two different experiences and shouldn't be confused as the same. While loneliness is upsetting and exhausting, times of stillness and solitude allow us to look inward for peace and res-toration. There's a lot to be said for tranquility and the sense of overall relief that accompanies it. In the periods when you find yourself alone, why not try to be constructive? You can learn a great deal about yourself if you're open and willing to take the time to listen. As odd as it sounds, the path out of isolation and loneliness could very well start with spending some time by ourselves.

As we've discussed, when we aren't productive in some way during periods of alone time, we can slip into boredom and unfulfillment, which could then lead to adopting activities and behaviors that become negative addictions.

What if we reframed being by ourselves not as being lonely, but as being *privileged* enough to get to know ourselves better—privileged enough to come to an understanding of what we're seeking in life? By looking inward before assessing our connections with the world around us, we can concentrate on the "why" of our actions. Without outside interference or distractions, we can carefully consider our values and goals. Asking ourselves probing questions helps us have a better understanding of what may have happened to knock us off course or to have damaged or destroyed our secure bonds with others. The bad news is that our thoughts and actions have probably put us in this position, but the good news is that we and we alone have the power to change our circumstances and our thoughts. Others can provide support and understanding, but we have to do the heavy lifting required to create positive, lasting change in our lives and achieve meaningful connectedness.

A person doesn't need to face major life issues to reap the benefits of solitude because it can serve as a crucial developmental stage at any time. Being alone provides an opportunity to self-reflect and to troubleshoot the obstacles in our paths, which can improve the effectiveness of our decision making. This can be especially impactful early in life, when our personalities are still developing. For example, in asserting the need for privacy, teenagers can secure time by themselves to process and understand their thoughts and emotions. It allows them to avoid the judgments of others and to perform essential introspection. This is also true for adults—just ask any mother how valuable a little me time is!

No matter how busy our schedules become, it's never a waste of time to set aside periods of solitude because they can have a positive reframing effect on our mindset. There's a lot to be said for regularly removing ourselves from social pressures and the judgment of others. Doing so will make us feel less self-conscious, and this sense of relief will frequently allow us to gain confidence in our ability to navigate difficult situations without having to always rely on social support. Freeing ourselves from the constraints of social interactions has been shown to provide a multitude of benefits:

Calmness. We've all heard the phrase "being comfortable in your own skin," and spending time alone allows us to do just that. Without the distraction of outside influences, we can be at ease and gain insight into who we are as individuals.

Empathy. Solitude gives us a chance to remove ourselves from family, coworkers, and circles of friends to consider perspectives that may be outside the views of those groups. It provides an opportunity to develop a better understanding of and more compassion for people who possess viewpoints that are different from ours.

Production. Being continually surrounded by others diminishes personal productivity, especially in the workplace. A bit of privacy goes a long way when it comes to concentration and focus.

Creation. By removing outside distractions for periods of time, we allow our thoughts the opportunity to roam freely, which tends to spark creativity.

Planning. Setting aside some quiet time gives us an occasion to evaluate our work and activities and to assess our current and future goals. It also lets us consider the necessary changes we need to make to get to where we want to be in life.

Happiness. Solitude may be just as necessary as meaningful relationships with others. Studies have shown that it improves stress management, overall life satisfaction, and overall happiness.

To an extent, the demands of your overall life situation and lifestyle will determine how much time you can carve out for yourself. This doesn't mean, however, that you shouldn't make it a priority. Just as you would set aside time to go to the gym for a workout, schedule an afternoon away from the distractions in your life to reflect, recharge, and regroup. The clarity and understanding you'll achieve during these times will allow you to return to the hustle and bustle of life reenergized and revitalized.

There's no doubt that the remedy for loneliness is devoting time and effort to building (or rebuilding) secure and supportive relationships with others. But before you can do this, you need to get yourself on track and attune with yourself. If you can establish a sense of serenity by being alone, then you can bring yourself back to this calming place when tough moments arise in your life. Align yourself first so that you know you have a stable foundation on which to build.

Your Thoughts and Emotions

A vital part of the process of connecting with yourself is identifying your feelings and reactions so you can adequately address and nurture your overall needs. Self-reflection is crucial to better recognition and understanding of what makes us who we are as individuals. It allows us to consider the components of our psychological makeup.

During times of self-reflection, it's also beneficial to consider the concept of *attunement*. When most of us think about "tuning in" to something, we envision radio and television stations rather than our own mind, body, and spirit. But the process of emotional attunement is a vital practice that can assist us in detecting, listening to, and adjusting to our inner voice and the messages our bodies are sending out.

Many stress-related issues and physiological problems can be dealt with if we're proactive and in touch with our bodies. Attunement is key in building empathy for others. It influences how we react to their emotional needs and behavior. I also believe that you can and should self-attune as a necessary building block in connecting to yourself.

How will you develop the ability to convey feelings and emotions if you're unable to listen to, identify, and understand your own? Being able to process and genuinely appreciate your feelings, needs, and wants in our fast-paced society is something that takes a high level of effort and focus. Self-attuning is an area that I believe the majority of us can significantly improve on.

In all my years of practice, I've never had someone come to me and say, "You know, I'm already very comfortable in my skin. Can you help me to feel a little *more* comfortable?" In fact, it's quite the opposite!

I'm reminded of Matthew, who was fifty-four years old when he first came to see me. He was overweight and suffered from depression. In addition to having difficulty dealing with his weight issues, he wrestled with a profound feeling of inadequacy. As a young boy growing up in Minnesota, he recalled his mother being quite harsh in her criticisms of him. His father was often out of town working, so Matthew was raised primarily by his mom. Nothing he did was ever good enough. He was an only child, and the harder he tried to please her, the more displeasure he incurred.

Matthew admitted that he had a recurring dream of going through a room with many doors. No matter which door he opened, there was nothing there. He constantly hoped that something would be behind the door, such as a solution to a problem. The nothingness of it all increased his feelings of despondency during his waking hours. He was a very bright, intuitive man who had spent a considerable amount of time working with a Jungian therapist, and became conversant with the myths Jung developed.

Years after that work, Matthew felt profoundly dissatisfied with himself. He felt out of touch with his body. The harder he tried to lose weight, the more it crept up on him. Eventually, Matthew and I were able to look at his dreams and some of the things he was doing that were self-destructive and affecting his work. He had a very important leadership role on a local community board but that position came with a bittersweet price, as many of his colleagues were dismissive of him. This negative feedback from others caused him a great deal of distress.

Although Matthew had a few good friends, at the end of the day, he would take solace in food. I recall him saying, "I'm going to Italy and I'm going to eat pasta, okay?" I looked at him with a twinkle in my eye and said, "It's up to you." Unsurprisingly, Matthew came back from his trip a few pounds heavier.

In therapy, we worked assiduously on his relationships with his mother and with himself, while also determining what kinds of things he needed to feel comfortable in his own skin. Until those things were done, we wouldn't get very far. While he was in therapy, Matthew wrote a brilliant book that was later published. It was quite paradoxical that he could be so astute as a professional but the opposite in his personal life.

Matthew's story isn't an isolated one, however. Most people are composed of a series of paradoxes such as the ones identified below by therapist, author, and speaker Esther Perel:

I want closeness, but I also want space.

I want intimacy, but I also wish to have independence.

I want to love, but I also want to lust.

I want to be monogamous, but I also want to have an affair.[1]

The paradoxes that comprise the human condition are something that we need to address and manage. Many options are available when it comes to the choices we make, which is why we have such difficulty choosing. In short, we want a little of everything!

Meditation

One of my favorite ways to get in touch with myself is the practice of mediation. It intentionally turns our attention away from distracting thoughts and toward a single point of reference. For example, meditation can focus on our breath, bodily sensations, compassion, or specific thoughts. Research shows that meditation elevates mood, increases concentration, and enhances feelings of social connection. It's vital to spend at least ten minutes per day meditating, or at the very least, reflecting.

I reflect every morning; rather, I sit with a double espresso in my hand and watch the dawn break before I see my first patient at 8:00 a.m. I pause and allow myself to feel humbled, excited, and grateful for the work that I'm about to do. I take these moments to feel appreciation for the life I've been given and the things that I feel passionate about. I reflect on what I might do that day to show kindness—not in my work but in my personal life. I think about community—my village, as it were—and how to get in touch with others, perhaps not today but in the next few days. *Village* for me means my community, my people, and my friends who have become my family. *Village* means being concerned as well with the larger picture, the global picture, and what I might do in a minuscule way to help with urgent issues such as climate change, violence, cruelty, and narcissism. What do I do? What can I do? I allow thoughts and emotions to surface without judgment in answer to those questions.

Setting a timer helps this reflective process, because when the timer rings, I stop. Otherwise, I'm sure that I could sit there for a very long time feeling incredibly comfortable!

I usually start with breathing. Once I've finished my coffee, I inhale through my nose to the count of four and exhale through my mouth to another four count, readjusting my body as I do so. I then get in touch with a higher being, with the philosophical issues on my mind. I've done this nearly all my life, from the time I was about thirteen onward. I just didn't know that the word for what I was doing was *meditation*. I would sit quietly and think about things in the morning. That's a pattern that has continued consistently throughout my life.

My mantra is usually "Do no harm." This is very important to me, and I always set about keeping to this motto. Many people would agree that mindfulness goes a long way toward that.

I think that if you try doing this basic meditation exercise on your own, you'll accomplish amazing results.

Try asking yourself: "What three things do I want to do today with excellence? What one thing do I choose to do with mediocrity?" By deliberately choosing one thing to do with mediocrity, you give yourself permission to be less of a perfectionist.

Then think about yesterday and what went well and why. It's a continuous feedback process. For me, it's just about being surprised by the thoughts that turn up.

What lies behind us and what lies before us are tiny matters compared to what lies within us.
–Henry S. Haskins

Self-Care

There is no more critical connection in life than that between the mind and the body. Developing the skill required to read your body's physical and emotional cues is vital to your overall happiness and well-being. Real problems arise when we choose to ignore the body's obvious signals. When your mind and your body are at odds with each other, a state of disharmony sets in. Paying attention to your body requires patience, concentration, and dedication, but when you truly listen, you'll realize that your body wants to be your friend, not your enemy.

The first thing most of us neglect when we're overworked and overextended is self-care. It's easy to get caught up in the hustle and bustle of life and forget to listen to what our bodies tell us daily. For example, you're inundated at work, and you feel as if you don't have a moment of free time in your schedule. Because your days have become so hectic and you can barely keep up with the pace, you don't eat right, quit working out, and slip into other "comforting" negative habits. You reduce the amount of time you spend asleep, and the sleep you do get is often restless. Before you know it, you become lonely and isolated and have stopped interacting with your friends and family. It's easy to remain on autopilot for a while. Eventually, though, you'll reach a point of diminishing returns where everything you attempt becomes counterproductive. This is when you know it's time to hit the reset button and start all over again. Some cues are easier to pick up on than others, but either way, you need to listen.

What are some of the ways in which you ignore your body's cues?

How do you know when you're uptight?

How do you know when you're stressed out?

Can you pinpoint where you hold tension in your body?

Sleep

The body is a finely tuned piece of machinery that needs to be maintained in order to function properly. I often ask my patients questions such as, "If you owned an expensive vehicle, would you fill the gas tank with sugar? Would you set out to work in the morning with a phone whose battery is charged to only ten percent?" The obvious answer to both questions is no. But we seem to have no problem doing exactly those things

Exercise

According to therapist, author, and speaker Esther Perel, from the moment we enter the world, we have two sets of human needs: 1) the need for security, safety, predictability, and belonging; and 2) the need for adventure, mystery, exploration of the unknown, autonomy, freedom, and love. Some people emerge from childhood favoring their needs for security and protection, while others come out seeking space, freedom, choice, and self-expression.

Think of a moment when you felt secure, content, satisfied—a moment perhaps when you were being held, a moment when you felt "I'm good enough" or "I'm safe." When you had that moment, what stood out for you? How did you experience it in your body? What did it feel like when you were enveloped in safety and security?

Next, think of another moment when you took a risk and ventured into the unknown outside your comfort zone. It should be a time when you risked being seen even though you're imperfect. Maybe you were standing up for yourself. Perhaps you spoke up when you usually wouldn't. What was it like to be on that side? How does your body experience itself when it's being bold and adventurous? Were you scared or anxious?

We all have a need for predictability and belonging, but we also require adventure, novelty, mystery, and risk-taking. The point of this exercise is to compare the ways you processed both experiences: the experience of safety and the experience of risk. How did each one feel for you? The exercise can also help us understand that we have both sets of needs—for predictability and belonging and also for adventure, novelty, surprise, mystery, and risk-taking.

to our bodies by getting very little sleep each night. We treat our bodies as if they were slaves, forcing them to accept the abuse we dish out. Today, we often care for our digital devices better than ourselves. For example, what do you do with your smartphone every night before you go to bed? You plug it in to recharge the battery, of course. In fact, you panic if you forget to charge it. And yet we go through the majority of our day feeling run-down and fatigued, never catching up on lost sleep or recharging our own batteries. We cannot function at our highest and best levels when we're sleep deprived. There's no getting around it. Our bodies need rest to repair and restore. Research has shown that the disruption of sleep can cause havoc in the mind by impairing our thinking and development of emotions. It also affects levels of stress hormones such as cortisol, and of neurotransmitters.[2] Various studies estimate that up to 90 percent of adult and child patients with significant depression experience some type of sleep problem, which only increases the likelihood that their depression will worsen. Sleep problems not only can have a drastic effect on moods and emotions but can also contribute to the relapse of negative addictions.

CATEGORIES OF SLEEP

Typically, every ninety minutes or so, we cycle between two major types of sleep: REM and quiet. As rest progresses, the length of time we spend in either type changes.

1. **REM (RAPID EYE MOVEMENT) SLEEP** refers to the period of sleep when we tend to dream. Our breathing, blood pressure, heart rate, and body temperature increase close to the levels they typically occupy when we're awake. REM sleep has been shown to contribute to our emotional well-being and to improve learning and memory function.

2. **QUIET SLEEP** refers to the period when we advance through the four stages of increasingly deep sleep. Our breathing and heart rate slow, our muscles relax, and our body temperature drops. The physiological changes that occur during the deepest stage of quiet sleep help boost our immune system.

Good mental health and adequate rest are directly connected. Depriving yourself of the sleep your body requires can have severe consequences for your physical and psychological well-being. A lack of sleep can eventually contribute to severe psychiatric difficulties. At the same time, those with mental problems are more likely to suffer from insomnia (difficulty falling or remaining asleep), and therefore it's possible to fall into a vicious cycle in which one continuously feeds the other.

Those with preexisting psychiatric conditions suffer the worst, and lack of rest only compounds the problem. People dealing with things such as depression, anxiety, bipolar disorder, and attention deficit hyperactivity disorder (ADHD) are particularly susceptible to sleep difficulties. Consider these two statistics: nearly 18 percent of the US population chronically struggles with sleep, and nearly 80 percent of patients in common psychiatric practices are known to suffer the same. For many years, we've considered conditions such as insomnia and other sleep disorders to be symptoms of mental disorders, but recent research suggests that sleep problems directly contribute to and possibly raise the risk of those disorders. Kahneman et al.[3] followed the daily moods of 909 female workers. What do you think correlated most strongly with happiness? Was it job benefits? Income? No—it was sleep quality.

We see it more and more: a lack of quality sleep is associated with a tendency toward depression.

Improving Rest

Most sleep problems and insomnia are generally treated in the same way for all patients, regardless of whether they suffer from psychiatric disorders. The fundamentals of treatment can range from one to a combination of lifestyle changes, including psychotherapy, behavioral strategies, and medications. If you're looking for ways to improve your rest, here are a few things to consider:

Increase Physical Activity. Exercising regularly and engaging in aerobic activity help people fall asleep quicker, spend more time in deep sleep, and wake fewer times over the course of the night. Exercise energizes the body, so it shouldn't be done immediately prior to going to sleep.

Practice Good Sleep Hygiene. *Sleep hygiene* refers to different practices you can employ in order to sleep better, including:

—Keep the bedroom dark and free from distractions, especially television or computers.

—Use the bedroom only for sleeping, daytime naps, and having sex.

—Try to stay awake longer to ensure that sleep is more restful.

—Keep to a routine sleep-and-wake schedule.

Limit Nicotine, Caffeine, and Alcohol. Most of us are well aware that caffeine is a stimulant and can contribute to both restlessness and sleeplessness, but it's also important to note that nicotine and alcohol can have the same effects on our bodies as well. At first, our nervous systems are depressed by alcohol, and we can easily fall asleep. Once the effects wear off later in the night, however, we become restless and frequently wake up. Nicotine increases our heart rate and speeds up our thinking, which can also make it challenging to rest. Ideally, it's better to give up these substances entirely, but if you do choose to use them, be sure you don't do so too close to bedtime.

Employ Relaxation Techniques. In order to help calm racing thoughts, stress, and anxiety, try techniques such as deep breathing, guided imagery, and meditation. There are many apps available to assist you through the process. My favorites are Calm and Headspace, but there are plenty of others from which to choose.

Maintain a Nutritious Diet. Establishing a healthy eating regimen is important. Notice how your mood and energy levels elevate when you eat clean foods and properly hydrate with water. My patients often increase their life satisfaction by simply eliminating added sugar and processed foods from their diets.

By connecting with ourselves, we can help create lives that are fulfilling and meaningful. The more we get to know ourselves, the more empowered we feel. Happiness is directly tied to connection, whether it be with others or ourselves. Once we try it, we want to connect more. In fact, we can't wait to connect!

You are very powerful, provided
you know how powerful you are.
— Yogi Bhajan

chapter six

··

CONNECTING WITH OTHERS

The opposite of addiction isn't sobriety, it's connection.
—JOHANN HARI

first heard this quote by Johann Hari when I watched his Ted Talk, "Everything You Think You Know about Addiction Is Wrong." Wow, did he have it right! Over the years, I, too, have found through my patients that addiction is rarely about the pleasure or effects of the substances they numb themselves with; what's really going on is that they've become incapable of connecting with others. Connection is healthy and essential to our well-being. Without it, it's impossible to achieve a true state of happiness. Robert Weiss, PhD, sums it up best by saying, "Addiction is not a substance disorder, it's a social disorder."[1]

I remember that, for the first two decades of my life, I had an incredible amount of fun learning; though it was only upon attending university that I felt for the first time that I really fit in. Then, when I earned my doctorate at the University of Toronto, I was delighted because, in addition to excelling academically and socially, I was also the president of the International Students Association. I had found my niche in life and had the opportunity to study something that I was passionate about. I met people with whom I could connect. They call Toronto a meeting place, and for me, it was where I met my soul. It was there that I got in touch with who I am, perhaps for the first time in my life. This felt liberating. I was proud of my accomplishments but also of the deep connections I had made. Whether I was helping international students get to know their peers better or just enjoying a night out with close friends, the connection felt right.

Now that we've reached inward and hopefully identified and understand how we process many of our feelings and emotions, it's time to start reaching outward to establish or reestablish meaningful connections with others. Healthy relationships improve our mental health and lower rates of morbidity and mortality. They have the power to inspire and aid us in learning, growing, and discovering purpose and meaning in our lives.

As we continually negotiate between our needs for togetherness and for freedom, our needs for love and for desire, and our needs for security and for adventure, we pick people who match our vulnerabilities and bring them into our lives. Our relationships determine who we are because we're social animals. The way others relate to us will yield, to a certain extent, a feeling of connectedness and a significant reduction of loneliness. If a person has a good self-image, a strong network of friends, and connections with his or her peer group at work, chances are that these things will provide a buffer against loneliness. In fact, there's a trend in the UK among people who retire, and among the elderly in general, to get involved in social groups—for example, walking groups, book clubs, or mentoring groups in which they become surrogate grandparents to younger children. In Japan, adolescents are encouraged to teach the elderly how to become more computer literate.

As tricky as socializing can be when you're overwhelmed by stress, anxiety, and feelings of loneliness, it's a crucial component of recovery.

From Stress to Strength

Take a moment to consider the events of a typical day. We interact with the physical world (people, places, and things) around us and process external stimuli. When these experiences are removed, our thoughts can quickly turn inward and profoundly alter our state of mind. Without others to exchange ideas and emotions with, we become uneasy and uncertain of our surroundings, especially when we're alone. We can quickly become stressed out and anxious about, well, *everything*. Without anyone else around to share and process information with, our thoughts can rapidly turn dark. The ensuing loneliness and feelings of depression make it difficult to initiate contact with others.

What if I told you that worry, anxiety, and stress could actually work *for you* in building meaningful connections? Well, as unlikely as it seems, they certainly can!

Once again, it all comes back to how you think about and process your emotions. How you interpret stress as an emotional and physical signal makes all the difference in the effect it will have on you. The ongoing battle to handle it is something every one of us faces. A great deal can be accomplished if we can change our mindset when assessing the role that stress plays in our lives, and if we can adjust our responses.

We experience stress as either a threat or a challenge. If we're fortunate enough to have the resources to cope with it, then we can consider it a "stress challenge." But if we don't have an adequate support system and find the situation to be too difficult, we see it as a "stress threat." While challenges typically energize and inspire us, threats can cause us to retreat and often inhibit our progress in many different ways—and the longer the threat lingers, the greater the chances of harm to our health from elevated stress levels. This is why it's notably important to find a way to pursue opportunities for positive change. As hard as it can be to try to socialize when you're feeling down, it's a necessary step toward living a less lonely existence.

In her book *The Upside of Stress: Why Stress Is Good for You, and How to Get Good at It*, author Kelly McGonigal notes the benefit of the body's release of oxytocin as a part of the stress response. This feel-good chemical is released by our pituitary glands and serves many functions, such as increasing our threshold for pain, reducing our cortisol levels, and lowering our blood pressure. But it also motivates us to seek the support of positive social interactions in difficult times. McGonigal describes human connections as "a built-in mechanism for stress resilience."[2] I love that, don't you?

So, the next time you feel defeated and stressed out, attempt to reframe your response from dread to anticipation.

Your body's release of adrenaline and oxytocin can motivate you to take action instead of overwhelming you and causing you to shut down. You can utilize the feelings associated with loneliness as a springboard to propel yourself into increased connectivity. Instead of closing yourself off from others, find a way to use stressful times as an opportunity to open yourself up.

The longer a person experiences loneliness, the more difficult it is to reestablish connection with others. Don't spend another moment considering when the right time to connect should be. The time is now!

Reaching Out: Identifying Reconnections and New Connections

Navigating the treacherous pathway out of loneliness is not a passive endeavor. It's undoubtedly a daily grind that requires consistent effort and attention to get and remain connected. The good news is that no matter how lonely or isolated you may feel, you aren't starting from zero. There are probably many positive relationships in your life that you may be overlooking or have just lost touch with. It's helpful to concentrate on reopening the lines of communication with current friends and family before moving on to building new relationships. To some degree, we all have people in our lives whom we can reach out to. The choice to do so is usually up to us, and so we need to be willing to take the first step.

Who have you lost connection with? Who do you stalk on social media even though you never reach out? Who are the people with whom you would like to reconnect?

The people you choose—and it is a *choice*—to bring into your life should be positive, reliable, and trustworthy. The last things you need in a time of loneliness and disconnection are people who will have a negative influence on you and disrupt the process of connection you're attempting to achieve.

So, if there's a chasm between your current behavior and where you would like to be, how do you go from a self-limiting mindset of "I can, I should, but I'm not" to "Here is where I need to be"?

The bridge, in my estimation, is motivation!

Building new relationships isn't as simple as surrounding yourself with other people. Many people hold themselves back because they don't want to put in the work of socialization. Small talk bores them, they find new environments uninteresting, and they generally don't care. But they should. Connection is the antidote to loneliness. Without it, stress levels rise and feelings of disconnection worsen.

Many of us have at one time or another been surrounded by people and still felt a sense of isolation. Why? The likelihood is that we weren't invested in those relationships. There could be myriad reasons for that, but most often it's because we weren't achieving an emotional or social connection. So, the goal is to identify and establish meaningful relationships with others, and to do so in the right environment.

In his book *The Great Good Place*, author Ray Oldenburg emphasizes the importance of finding a "third place," or an environment outside the home (the "first place") and the workplace (the "second place") that allows a person to meet and connect with others. Oldenburg defines this as somewhere "you relax in public, where you encounter familiar faces, and make new acquaintances."[3] It could be anywhere people frequently gather, such as restaurants, coffee shops, parks, community centers, or fitness clubs. Is there an environment you routinely visit where you can be social and connect with others? Of course, in the age of COVID-19, extra precautions need to be taken in choosing safe places. If your community still has heavy restrictions, such interactions may need to remain online for a while. You can still connect on Instagram, Twitter, Snapchat, Facebook, and the like. Ironically, I used to have reservations about the digital world because of the physical distance I thought it was putting between people, but now I recognize the role it has played in bringing us together during these unprecedented times.

The most important thing is that we establish a sense of belonging with others who share similar beliefs or interests. The difference is whether we're emotionally engaged or not.

Personally, some of the happiest moments of my life are when I connect with others, be they at work with a patient or with a friend or loved one in my personal life. Those connections are so important, because then I no longer feel loneliness. Instead, I feel visible and present. I'm a participant in life and not an observer. For instance, when I'm with Ingrid, a friend who has the most positive energy, just being able to be there and connect with her is enough to leave me feeling ecstatic. To see the glimmering of joy on her face makes me happy. At times I would go visit Ingrid after an exhausting day at work, but once I was there in the moment with her, my fatigue would leave me and I would be jubilant as I returned home. This notion of connecting with others, like I do with Ingrid, is paramount to me. I believe it to be one of the most important ways in which human beings can achieve that feeling we got when, in years gone by, we lived in villages and were so closely connected with one another. It was as though we had the same pulse, the same heartbeat. We were totally attuned to one another, very much like the way a mother is to her child.

Social Media

Evolutionary anthropologist Robin Dunbar has established an approximate cognitive limit to the number of friends with whom we can maintain stable social relationships. This limit—150 people—is known as "Dunbar's number." The number isn't meant to put a cap on the total number of people we can know; rather, it covers those with whom we can be genuinely empathetic, supportive, and trusting.

So, what does this imply as far as all our hundreds or, in some cases, thousands of social media connections are concerned? What does "connecting" actually mean in the age of social media? Is it possible to have friends whom we never meet in person? For example, should we consider Facebook friends to be "real" friends? According to Dunbar's number, social media platforms can't expand our social circles because our brains are incapable of coping with such large groups of people. Still, it isn't the same for everyone, and your situation will depend on your individual needs and expectations. As mentioned earlier, having these connections, to whatever degree of intimacy they fulfill, has been a saving grace for many when they've been unable to get out and socialize in person.

Marilyn was a twenty-nine-year-old woman who was addicted to social media. The first thing she did upon waking was to check her devices to see what other people were doing, and

Whether or not you use social media regularly, it's essential to remember that true friendship and meaningful connections are about understanding and support, not merely a number on a social media platform. The question isn't *who* you connect with but *how* you connect with them.

- Can you count on one of your social media "friends" in a time of need?
- Do your social networking contacts really care if you have a bad day?
- Does social media constitute a genuine human exchange of emotions and ideas, or is it a form of avoidance that offers us momentary comfort and relief?
- By relying on our digital devices, are we avoiding real human exchange?
- Is social media a solution for being disconnected, or does it merely *feel* like a solution?
- You use only two out of your five senses to connect with others through social media. Is this effective? Is it fulfilling?
- Do you feel as if you're investing enough face-to-face time with your friends, coworkers, and family?

then she would negatively compare herself to them. Other people always seemed to have more interesting lives. They seemed to have better clothes, better figures, and more engaging careers.

"What's the matter with me?" Marilyn asked me. "Why can't I be like them?"

When I asked her what she thought would happen if she didn't go on social media for a day, Marilyn was aghast. She looked at me in shock and said, "Are you kidding me? I need to do that. Otherwise, how will I know what's going on?"

When I asked her to tell me what social media did for her, she pointed out that it helped her select clothing and accessories to purchase; from the way she presented, it was clear that she believed in buying the best designer label shoes, apparel, or handbags she could afford. She said she learned through social media how to look good. "Good" in this context, of course, meant measuring up to whomever she saw on posts—actors, models, famous musicians, or other figures in popular culture.

"What does that really do for you?" I pressed.

"Well, it gives me a benchmark," she said. "It tells me how I should live."

"Does it make you happy?"

"No," she said. "But that's not the point. I'm not happy, but I don't think it's because of social media. It's just because I'm not as good as those people."

Marilyn had worked assiduously at learning to be happy, but she hadn't *felt* happy for years. This was a result of her not believing that she measured up to other people. During childhood, she compared herself to others and found that there was always someone who was better than she was scholastically, physically, or in terms of popularity.

"What about relationships?" I asked.

"Well," she said, "that's another problem. It's hard."

Marilyn had had several relationships that didn't work for her. She felt that the men she'd dated objectified her. They didn't see her for who she really was but rather for the way that she presented, which she'd learned from social media.

Through therapy, Marilyn eventually got to the point where she could give herself permission to remove herself from social media. At first she disengaged only for a day or so; then she tried four days to check how she felt. After that, she was regularly disengaging for two weeks at a time.

Marilyn eventually found that without social media, her life satisfaction increased. Initially, she felt scared that she would miss out on important details because she'd grown so used to routinely checking in. Disengaging was a long process for her, and it didn't happen automatically. Automaticity doesn't occur with such a compulsion. But it was important for her to learn to check in with herself rather than to check herself against others. Marilyn took thirty days away from social media to break the habit. She replaced it with savoring her coffee in the morning and being mindful. "I'm creating the gospel according to me," she said playfully.

It's not only about the various sites and applications people use to compare themselves against others but also about when and where they use their devices to do so.

I recently had a patient who was severely obese, as were his wife and two daughters. When I asked him what they did for exercise, he replied, "Well, we're a tablet family."

Because of my British background, I assumed that when he said "tablet," he was referencing a pill. I actually thought to myself, "I wonder what type of medication they're taking."

I looked at him with some confusion and said, "Tablet? Help me to understand."

"We're all on our devices during supper," he answered.

"*Oh*. I see," I said. "Have you read the Canadian food guide?"

"No."

"The Canadian food guide states that you shouldn't eat alone. Instead of isolating, you ought to interact and talk with people."

While my response may have been a scathing indictment of his practices, by no means is this story unique. It's far too common, in fact. Our relationship with our devices is a woeful commentary on our society, our loneliness, and our disconnection.

Being Open and Forthcoming

A lonely person usually behaves in a less friendly way than a happier, more fulfilled person. They're generally closed off and refrain from exhibiting signs that might encourage others to approach them. How often do you engage in activities and share your personal feelings with others? Self-disclosure plays an essential role in relieving stress and establishing healthy relationships.

Ask yourself this: What am I contributing to social situations? It's important to take time to consider how others perceive you and how your behavior is being accepted, rejected, or denied. Sharing with and opening up to others is a great way to break the ice. By establishing a common ground on which to interact, you help others to identify with your situation. We've discussed getting in tune with your emotions, needs, and wants. Now, what about being in tune with these same things in other

people? If you don't make an effort, it's going to be challenging to make connections and sustain relationships. Be active and express yourself. Don't be afraid to convey your thoughts and emotions to others by opening your heart.

The Way You Respond

Parenting 101 is teaching our children that it's not *what* they say so much as *how* they say it. This philosophy carries over into everyday life. Have you ever considered your tone? Do you always convey the message you intend, or has your delivery ever stood in your way? What about your body language—do you subtly mirror the person you're connecting with? How do you react when people close to you give you good news? Are you genuinely excited for them? Do you respond effusively and sincerely? How about when they share bad news? Are you empathetic? Do you offer a shoulder to lean on?

Relationships are a two-way street; you get what you give. So, opening up and sharing our lives is only half of the process. You must also consider the receiving component of the process—in other words, how you listen and react to others when they share news matters. The way you react to the thoughts and feelings of others can be either beneficial or detrimental to the bond you're attempting to create.

Here are some typical ways in which we react.

1. THE ACTIVE AND CONSTRUCTIVE RESPONSE

There's a reason people relay their good news to others; they want them to share in the joy of the moment. The ability to express authentic interest in what others disclose to you and to

The next time someone shares news with you, think about how you're responding.

—Is your attention focused on them or on you?

—Are you genuinely curious about the circumstances of their story and conveying authentic interest?

—Are you genuinely happy or sad for them, or are you passive, dismissive, or ready to steer the conversation back to your feelings and needs?

—Be mindful of your body language and physical positioning when you give and receive information. Are you maintaining eye contact? Are you facing people and giving them your full attention? Or are you conveying boredom or distraction? This even applies to FaceTime or Zoom calls; keep your eyes on those you are talking to and not on your own onscreen image!

respond in encouraging ways is what psychologist Shelly Gable calls "Active and Constructive Responding."[4] It's a powerful way to cultivate positive emotions and enhance relationships.

Suppose a close friend or family member comes to you and says they're pregnant. An active and constructive reaction to this news could be, "That's wonderful! I know you're going to be an amazing parent. Let's make some plans for dinner to celebrate!" You're not only positively acknowledging this exciting development in their life but also conveying genuine interest in and authentic curiosity about the future of the situation. Think

about times when you or someone you know has responded this way. How did it make you feel?

2. THE ACTIVE AND DESTRUCTIVE RESPONSE

In this case, you react to the news, but instead of adding an active, elaborative component, you attach a negative outlook. To use the pregnancy example again, you might respond, "I hope you know what you're doing. Kids change everything, and you aren't going to be able to do most of the things you'd like to do in the future." This would be a quick and not-so-subtle way to, as they say, rain on someone's parade. Think about times when you or someone you know has responded this way. How did it make you feel?

3. THE PASSIVE AND CONSTRUCTIVE RESPONSE

This typically subdued reaction involves little or no emotion. It remains positive but falls short of elaboration. For instance, "Oh, good for you." Although you aren't being outwardly negative, you also aren't providing the other person with positive reinforcement to advance the conversation. Think about times when you or someone you know has responded this way. How did it make you feel?

4. THE PASSIVE AND DESTRUCTIVE RESPONSE

On the flip side of the Active and Constructive coin is the Passive and Destructive response. This type of reaction is the least effective in building connections. It contains no excitement or affirming information, and in this case would sound something like, "Okay. I'm starving; let's go grab something to eat." You're mostly ignoring everything the other person has conveyed and are blowing them off. Without question, this is the most destructive response when it comes to the forming of a bond. You should try to avoid this type of reaction if you're determined to establish or reestablish relationships with those around you. It displays a total lack of interest in and respect for what the other person is offering. Think about times when you or someone you know has responded this way. How did it make you feel?

These reactions also include nonverbal communication cues. The active responses are usually accompanied by eye contact and/or a smile, while the passive responses can involve eye-rolling, shaking your head, or no eye contact at all.

It's our responses that greatly influence how others feel in our presence. Even if we think we're being fulfilled by an exchange or a conversation, the other person may not be. Subdued responses that lack enthusiasm or emotion aren't going to inspire people to share their thoughts and feelings with us in the future.

If you truly want to connect with others, you need to achieve a certain level of self-awareness. Without evaluating your behavior and conduct from time to time, you may not even realize that you're acting in ways that undermine your efforts to connect with others. Furthermore, you won't have any idea why your attempts come up short and both parties leave exchanges unfulfilled.

When Oprah Winfrey spoke at the Stanford Graduate School of Business, she talked about the three things that all interpersonal exchanges boil down to:

- Did you hear me?
- Did you see me?
- Did what I say mean anything to you?

Isn't that fascinating? Everyone wants to feel acknowledged. It's a commonality we all share. The more you can do to fulfill this desire, the better your relationships will be.

My willingness to be intimate with my own deep feelings creates the space for intimacy with another.
— Shakti Gawain

Resist the Negative Reaction

Negative self-talk can hamper your progress and damage your mindset. Negativity can also show up when we interact with others and cause just as much damage to the connections we're attempting to establish. Responding passively or destructively to others is easy; all you have to do is remain dismissive and put little or no effort into your interactions. Truly listening, understanding, and providing positive, constructive feedback may take energy, but it will be beneficial for both sides.

So, when someone shares their thoughts and emotions with you, there's no need to be overly critical of what they offer even if you don't agree or understand where they're coming from. Everyone is entitled to their opinions and feelings. It doesn't make them wrong and you right, or vice versa. Think of it this way: they didn't decide to confide in you because they were looking for a critical response. They were seeking recognition and understanding, not ridicule. Resist the urge to be judgmental and make a concerted effort to offer, at the very least, a few positive words of support. After all, wouldn't you want them to do the same for you? Specific statements of praise go a long way! Also, don't dole out solutions unless the request is made, and even then, proceed with caution.

I define connection as the energy that exists between people when they feel seen, heard, and valued; when they can give and receive without judgment; and when they derive sustenance and strength from the relationship.
– Brené Brown

Maintaining Connection

Putting in the time to establish and strengthen connections by reaching out to others doesn't mean that stress and anxiety won't creep back into your life from time to time. These emotions can make it very difficult to consistently initiate contact with others. It's no secret that friendships and meaningful connections take work to maintain. They need to be nurtured and nourished to remain healthy and grow deeper over time. It's often easy to let things lapse and slip away due to lack of time and energy. We need to remind ourselves, however, that our friends are vital to our happiness and well-being.

For years, my husband and I lived in a gated community with about twenty-five homes. One day, I announced to our neighbors, "Come to our place for an open house." And with that, I became the resident social director. Several times a year, I would host a get-together. People had lived in that neighborhood for over twenty years and never took the time to meet one another until I brought everyone under one roof for an afternoon, establishing community and connection among us.

I eventually sold that home and moved, but upon arriving in my new neighborhood, I arranged another gathering. Of the fifty people who attended, almost all of them said what fun it was and offered to take a turn—round-robin hosting! My curiosity and desire to get to know these people helped assuage my anxiety about how it would turn out. I have a friend who had a similar idea about creating connections with her neighbors, but this time it was during the early stages of the stay-at-home orders. She arranged a Zoom party for her entire apartment complex. It was calming to know that others were close by even if they weren't out and about, and it helped those who lived by themselves to enjoy the company of others for the evening. It was a resounding success! We are relational beings, so it helped to be able to interact while also seeing one another's places.

These experiences reminded me that we're often so caught up in our personal worlds that we rarely look outside of them. This isn't to say that social networks can be established overnight, but opening the door is a vital first step in nearly every situation. The strongest relationships begin when we establish common ground and build out from there.

chapter seven

....

A BEND IN THE ROAD IS NOT THE END OF THE ROAD

*One who gains strength by overcoming obstacles possesses
the only strength which can overcome adversity.*
—ALBERT SCHWEITZER

Many self-help books are directed at breaking bad habits as opposed to examining the underlying obstacles or problems. I call this putting out fires without finding the arsonist. That's why it's crucial to look for what's beneath the habit and what you may be trying to avoid or confront. Bad habits take up a lot of mental space, so once you've figured out and dealt with some of what's underlying the harmful patterns, either through introspection or with the help of a friend or a therapist, you won't have to squeeze positivity into the tight spaces between negative impulses anymore.

But getting a handle on the underlying emotions that create roadblocks may be the most challenging part for many people. Honest self-appraisal is not a simple task, and those around us are often not that helpful. Generally, people say what they think we want to hear. We tend to listen to the good things about ourselves while focusing or obsessing internally on the negative things (even though we spend a lot of time avoiding them).

So, dealing with the underlying pain is undoubtedly a necessary step toward overcoming roadblocks. And that's what this chapter is all about—looking inward at something rather than spinning around in a circle.

Sometimes, no matter how much preparation, motivation, and action we've invested in an activity we thoroughly enjoy, we find ourselves running out of fuel and prematurely stopping our participation. We've all experienced this—we come flying out of the starting gate with excitement and enthusiasm for a healthy activity only to eventually find ourselves flagging and procrastinating. Before long, we discover that enjoyable activity has disappeared altogether from our lives.

If you're determined to develop and maintain healthy, happy habits but experience a lack of progress, attempt to take smaller steps toward your goal. It may be a good idea, for example, to reduce your expectations about the length of time you want to spend exercising, at least for the moment. Keep reminding yourself that it's okay to pursue your goals in your own style and at your own speed, rather than comparing yourself with others. There's no rush. The dramatic effects of fatigue and time constraints can be lessened by the decision to go slowly, and this will allow you to feel more prepared to move forward.

So, how do we deal with the things that threaten to derail our best intentions? How do we prepare for events that yank us out of our routine?

1. **ALLOW YOURSELF A REWARD.** Make a deal with yourself that if you engage in at least a part of your regular goal-directed activity, you can treat yourself to something of value to you.

2. **TEMPORARILY REDUCE EXPECTATIONS.** Allow yourself to do less than you had planned. Be clear with yourself that once the dust has settled, you'll return to the original plan. Remember, you can always build on small steps. For example, ten minutes of daily exercise is doable, but two hours is daunting and may be disruptive to your day.

3. **ALTER TODAY'S GOAL.** For today only, customize the activity to accommodate whatever is interfering. For example, if you're feeling under the weather, instead of using the treadmill, go for a walk. If you're unwell—say, down and out with a cold—listen to a podcast about something that inspires and motivates you.

So, what else can cause us to let our motivation slip away?

Simply put, we encounter roadblocks that we don't have the resilience or strength to overcome, so we lose interest and move on.

We need to remember that setbacks are a part of life for all of us. No one is immune. But knowing that these barriers exist enables us to deal with them more effectively, and remembering that success isn't ensured just because a realistic plan has been made helps us to avoid feeling ambushed.

*Obstacles are those frightful things you see
when you take your eyes off your goals.*
~ Henry Ford

Identifying Obstacles

Setbacks and failures happen, so plan for them. Any barrier or hurdle that gets in the way of an anticipated positive outcome can be managed, but for this to happen, the barrier first must be identified.

We'll highlight some typical obstacles here and make suggestions for how to overcome them so you can move ahead. There are many kinds of roadblocks on the path to success, and since those obstacles are usually personal to you and your lifestyle, self-awareness is key. Try to pinpoint what or who the roadblock serves by getting in your way. Remember that moving forward takes courage. It requires the confidence to be tough, to smile more, to fight harder, to be more open-minded, and to accept help when it's needed.

Take a moment to try to identify which roadblocks are relevant to you. You can't overcome what you don't see!

1. ENVIRONMENTAL ROADBLOCKS

There are situations that exist all around us that can interfere with our plans. Despite our good intentions, we overshop, overeat, or overreact, partly thanks to environmental forces such as round-the-clock access to online shopping and to malls where we can satisfy just about every possible commercial impulse; a plethora of food delivery options available at any time of day or night; or road rage or other public displays of anger. These forces can overwhelm us and get in the way of our success. And when we succumb to our old habits, we often experience self-criticism. We put ourselves down and resort to negative thinking: "I'm such a failure"; "I have no willpower"; "I'm selfish"; "I'm all words and no action." Environmental roadblocks can stir up familiar behaviors that sabotage our success.

Belinda wants to curb her spending habits and save for a summer vacation. Although she thinks of heading straight home after work, she stops at the mall to return an item she bought the week before. She sees a sale on tees that she can't resist. She buys one . . . or two . . . or three, then goes home, where she realizes she spent twice the cost of the item she returned. What is Belinda doing in a situation like this? She's using environmental stimuli to become a roadblock for herself.

George, an accountant, comes home and thinks, "I'll just have one glass of wine and then talk with my wife." Instead, he sits down and has a couple of glasses of wine, and is thus emotionally absent to his wife and family. The roadblock here isn't just the wine but George's justification for why he needs it: "I deserve it because I've had a really tough day." Additionally, the statement "I'll just have one" is clearly self-deception.

Lauren, a medical assistant, once said to me, "I really want to begin a healthier eating regimen, but things always get in the way." When I asked what things got in the way, she told me, "Well, you know, the candy at home . . . When I have a stressful day in the office with the doctors trying to sort out the things

I have to do and they don't seem to understand that I'm not Wonder Woman, I get so stressed out that I indulge, or I forget about lunch and just pick up a burger on the way home instead of making the healthy salad and tuna that I was thinking of doing when we talked last week."

In all three of these cases, the environment conspires with the person's bad habits to create a roadblock. Until you're aware of what your roadblocks are, you won't be able to do anything about them but simply respond to the stimulus like one of Pavlov's dogs. Once you've identified the enemy that can justify your bad behavior—the mall, stress at work, or alcohol—you can begin to overcome it.

2. HIDDEN FORCES

The second roadblock, hidden forces, may be more difficult to understand.

For example, hidden forces were at play when twenty-four-year-old Jordan tried to do well on the job site but continually fooled around and eventually got fired. This wasn't his initial plan, but the unconscious desire or need to fool around intervened. It's possible that on some level Jordan didn't want the job; his parents pressured him to take it, and therefore he set himself up for failure. His underlying disinterest in the job was the *hidden force* that caused the failure. Conscious self-examination of behaviors is required if hidden forces are to be identified and dealt with effectively. We're all subject to faulty perceptions, but ruthless self-appraisal can keep hidden forces in check. Find a friend with whom you can be open and work together to ferret out reasons for your not seeing things clearly and how you might deal with them.

The fact of the matter is that not many people will tell us the truth about ourselves. Our society seems to be engaged in a never-ending dance of deception. Few people will tell us what's really going on. Someone might say to their friend, "I think I need to lose weight," and the friend responds, "No, you don't. You're fine just the way you are."

Let's talk about the ways in which hidden forces work against us. I'm thinking now of Lisa, who came to see me a couple of years back and presented a particularly difficult case. She was convinced that she needed to lose weight, but every time she did, she would regain it, along with a couple of extra pounds. Lisa was a very attractive woman, then in her early forties. She had a healthy marriage and two young children, but didn't seem to be able to keep the weight off. It was clear that she was quite knowledgeable about nutrition and could probably teach the world how to eat healthfully. That wasn't the issue.

So, what was stopping her? What was the hidden force there?

Lisa mentioned that whenever she lost weight, her husband would bring home a cherry pie for her, which she would devour. But what did the cherry pie really symbolize? Well, earlier in her marriage, when her husband was trying very hard to establish himself in his career, she engaged in an extramarital affair. At that time, Lisa was very slim. She said to me one day, "You know what I think it is? It's like this: Tom, my husband, doesn't want me to lose the weight because he's scared that I'm going to have another affair. I may be scared of it myself, and that's why I can't seem to maintain the weight loss."

Then there's the story of Angie, a financial advisor who was married to a physician. She was in her early fifties when she came to see me. She was also concerned about some excess weight she was carrying around. When I asked her about it, she happily informed me that she would eat at her lover's house, then go home to her husband and eat a second meal with him, because she was scared that she would be caught. So, what is the hidden force there?

She was deceiving herself on several levels. Was the food a metaphor? And if so, for what? Why she was eating two meals? What was really going on in her life?

At a very young age, Angie's parents divorced because of her father's infidelity. In an ironic way, she was trying to protect herself from a divorce and from being left behind by having a backup plan that actually brought both prospects into her present situation. Once she realized what she was doing, she elected to end her affair and to pursue marital therapy.

3. QUESTS FOR PERFECTION

Another roadblock is the quest for perfection, which is an unhealthy pursuit. Striving for perfection is an everyday practice in North American culture. We discussed this earlier, but it bears repeating in this context. For most people, the way we look, how we're perceived by others, and how driven we are to be the best matter. This preoccupation keeps us believing in the idea that being flawless is more important than being authentic and expressing our true selves. Unfortunately, chasing perfection is like running toward a mirage in the desert: much like that false image, perfection is never quite within anyone's reach.

Even so, the *idea* of being perfect is hard to resist.

Why?

It's addictive.

We're creatures of habit who are never satisfied. And if we're the least bit competitive, we're always striving to be better.

There's no escaping the draw: we're bombarded every single day with endless messages about perfection in the media and from our family, friends, and colleagues. These messages not only feed our deepest insecurities but also encourage us to believe that we must be something more or different from who we presently are. That somehow, a shift away from our true selves would be *better*.

That's not to say that striving for excellence isn't a good thing. It certainly is, but as a result, a lot of people unfairly hold themselves to an impossible standard—one none of us can ever truly live up to. Nobody is perfect, yet perfectionists expect no less of themselves than perfection. Identification of this personality trait may be the first step toward improving the positivity of your mindset.

How many of you had parents who instilled in you the need to do everything perfectly? You know, the so-called Protestant work ethic. I would get my knickers in a knot every time I missed a perfect outcome. Have you ever done that? Gotten stuck in the inevitable postmortems? I'm no pathologist (which, by the way, is an excellent conversation stopper), but the forensics I would run on situations in which I felt I had underperformed were truly exhaustive. I would go over every could-have and should-have there was, even if nothing could have been done differently. The net effect of my obsessing was that I was guaranteed to feel two feet tall by the end of it! So, one day I decided that this love affair with perfection, which had only caused me grief, would end. Using the metaphor of an illicit tryst really nailed it for me; I wanted to be visible, not hidden away like a shameful secret. When I broke up with my perfectionistic traits, it felt like getting rid of my bra! I discovered that I could be a satisfier instead of a maximizer.

4. SELF-DECEPTION, RATIONALIZATION, AND EXCUSES

Self-deception refers to the tendency to rationalize errors, mistakes, or failures to follow through. It's a set of attitudes and behaviors that thwart accurate assessment of a situation and therefore prevent the determination and acceptance of personal responsibility.

Consider the person who wants to achieve some particular goal but complains that an unhappy childhood is getting in the way, or the individual who complains that his or her job is just too demanding to meet the goal of more family time; in these instances, those people fall prey to the self-deception roadblock.

Another form of self-deception involves minimization, in which a person downplays what must be done and what they can do. An example might be the would-be writer who is simply "writing for pleasure." Perhaps this person thinks that writing just one line is sufficient for a particular day, or maintains that after a few minutes of writing, brain fatigue makes any additional work impossible.

The core of self-deception is the denial of truth to such a degree that we fool ourselves into believing the lie. Studies show that the average person tells "little white lies" several times a day, but it's those small lies we tell ourselves that often cause the most significant problems. The reasons for this are many and range from minor issues of self-control to full-fledged out-of-control delusions.

Think about some of the lies you tell yourself. For example, "I'll just be on the computer for ten more minutes"—and two hours somehow pass! Or, "I'll only eat a couple of spoonfuls of ice cream"—and "magically" the quart is gone!

Richard, a fifty-five-year-old psychologist, expressed a wish to write a communication text for physicians. He enjoyed an excellent clinical practice and had an amazing reputation for being insightful. But despite his qualifications and desire to write, he procrastinated for many years. At one point, he got as far as penning a first draft with a colleague. He submitted it to Springer, a leading publisher of health care books, and was told that with a few more additions to the text it would be accepted. But from that point onward, he simply stopped working on the project. He created countless excuses and ultimately abandoned the manuscript entirely. When asked why, he replied, "I got hypnotized at a workshop and thought I needed to write this book."

The point is that we all share some of these habits, but creating a new practice to meet them can shift everything. Rather than asking yourself, "Why am I not following through?" ask, "How can I use this as a chance to really come to terms with myself on a deeper level and move forward?"

5. HOOKED BY CAPTIVATING ACTIVITIES

We're constantly surrounded by various distractions that vie for our attention. All kinds of activities can capture our imagination and seem seductive in the moment. They call to us: making a snack, having a beer, watching television, calling a friend, hopping on Facebook, and even cleaning. But what is the value of these distractions in the long run? How do they take up so much of our time? How do they interfere with our happiness?

Such impulses need to be accounted for by proper preparation so you aren't ambushed by them (or can't pretend you were). Set yourself up for success by changing your environment. It's essential to create more value-added activities to counterbalance the captivating ones. We're talking about spending time, so think about it that way: How do you want to spend your allotment? I believe time is the most valuable commodity we have. We can't control the number of hours, minutes, or seconds in our day, but we have total control over how we spend them. I always say, spend wisely!

6. THE VICIOUS CYCLE

We're all familiar with the feeling of being caught in a never-ending loop. This roadblock happens when complex, hidden forces create a self-reinforcing cycle from which it's difficult to escape. For example, a person who always wants to please others may, in fact, be treated with disrespect. Because someone who constantly tries too hard can be irritating, it causes the exact opposite of the intended effect. Thus, this strategy locks the person in a vicious cycle, which over time may accelerate as the attempts to please are repeated and even exaggerated, with increasingly negative consequences. Think about children and how they react when you don't respond the way they want you to. It's the same for adults who get stuck in this cycle.

Another common trigger for the vicious cycle is the constant worry about ending up alone. Pervasive anxiety on this level often keeps someone in a relationship for too long. When the person finally breaks free, the worry, which lives outside of the specific relationship, will likely lead to another, similar cycle. Why? Because worry about ending up alone sets the main direction on the compass, and that direction leads nowhere but in circles.

Avoiding Negative Self-Talk

One of the most substantial barriers to positive thinking is negative self-talk. It's easy to fall into a pattern of negative thinking, and it's a difficult routine to break. As human beings, we're programmed to be critical, and often, even though we've done nothing wrong, our minds will still end up dragging us down with harmful thoughts. This can cause us to feel indecisive, overly apologetic, and insecure, which can also lead to depression and various stress-related problems.

We're wired to trust what our brains tell us. After all, our thoughts and instincts keep us safe, attract us to others, and help us discover solutions to life's problems. Our minds are predisposed to establish associations between ideas, thoughts, actions, and results. But there are certain situations in which our brains develop incorrect connections between these things and provide us with misconceptions that lead to dysfunctional emotions, causing us to form irrational fears and negative beliefs.

The methods our minds use to convince us of something that isn't actually true are called *cognitive distortions*, the theory of which was first proposed by psychologist Aaron Beck in 1976 and later popularized by David Burns in the 1980s. We all possess these inaccurate thoughts that reinforce negative thinking and feelings. They're mistakes in reasoning that come across as authentic and rational but inhibit our ability to think positively and cause us to process situations incorrectly, leading to emotional distress. Self-awareness teaches us to recognize behaviors that create chaos in our lives without our even realizing it.

The key to changing these cognitive distortions is first to identify them. They come in various forms but are all false or inaccurate tendencies and patterns of thinking that can inflict psychological suffering.

Here are some common cognitive distortions:[1]

Polarized Thinking. Also referred to as "black-and-white" thinking, this occurs when you view situations only in absolutes. Without stopping to examine circumstances or consider nuances, you fall into automatic generalization. It's a mindset that may cause you to believe that if you fail at something, then you're going to fail at everything. A common polarized thought, for example, is, "I never do anything right." When you think in this way, you tend to use words such as *never, always, nothing,* and *everything.* People who adopt the role of victim in life tend to have this mindset, because they don't think they have any control over the negative things that happen to them.

Filtering. This mindset involves magnifying a negative detail while disregarding any positive aspects of a situation. In doing this, your emotional well-being suffers considerably, and your sense of reality becomes distorted to the point where positivity ceases to exist.

Labeling and Mislabeling. People who label or mislabel will habitually create inaccurate or negative classifications for themselves and others—for example, "I'm a hopeless failure." Labels used in this way don't separate the person from the action or consequence. "I'm a failure" puts you in a room and locks the door, whereas a statement such as, "That didn't turn out the way I had hoped it would" leaves room for examination and improvement.

Overgeneralization. This way of thinking arises when you concentrate on one or two experiences and decide that's the way it will be for you in the future in whatever situation you find yourself. Think of that friend who says they can't connect with others because they weren't understood in their early adulthood. The person's conclusion is, "Why bother connecting with others? They'll only misunderstand me. It's all a waste of time." They generalize that as a result of one or two painful experiences, this is their lot in life moving forward. They're really only trying to protect themselves by staying away from people; they make the assumption that all people will behave this way toward them, and that no one will take the time to get to know them.

Catastrophizing. Also referred to as "magnifying," this mode of thinking causes you to imagine the worst possible outcome in every situation no matter what. It leads to expecting that everything will be a total disaster and causes your mind to run wild with what-if scenarios whenever you hear about something terrible taking place. For instance, "What if I get into a car accident on the way to the store?" Catastrophizing also involves using unfortunate events to justify your negative mindset. You imagine and expect the worst possible scenario, causing a great deal of stress and anxiety.

Personalization. We've all heard the phrase "taking things personally" applied to certain situations. This way of thinking causes you to take *everything* personally. You personalize the actions of others to the point where you believe that everything they do is a direct reaction to you, and you view yourself as the cause of bad results that you aren't responsible for.

People who personalize their stressors tend to blame themselves for things over which they have no control. They blame themselves for the actions or feelings of others or blame others for their personal feelings. For example, when someone who personalizes situations is laid off because of economic downsizing, they're apt to feel as if the loss of employment is due to poor job performance, when in fact it may simply be because they were the last to come on board, so logically they're the first to be let go. Personalization tends to be not only inaccurate but also extremely stressful.

Emotional Reasoning. Just because you feel a certain way about something doesn't mean it's true. Although this seems easy to identify and avoid, it's a distortion that people routinely encounter in their daily lives. It occurs when you turn your feelings about something into fact.

Emotional reasoners will consider their emotions about a situation to be evidence that they're right about a matter, rather than objectively examining the facts. Jumping to conclusions is an example of emotional reasoning. For an emotional reasoner, "I'm angry at you" is never the end of the sentence; rather, this statement is followed by an implication, ". . . therefore you have to be in the wrong." Acting on emotional reasoning will always exacerbate problems, not solve them.

It isn't easy to come to terms with the fact that you may not only *have* irrational thoughts or beliefs but that you could also be unknowingly *reinforcing* them over time. But rest assured that all of us have become entangled in a few cognitive distortions at one time or another. This isn't to say that you'll fall prey to distorted thinking on a daily basis, but it's nearly impossible to avoid entirely. The important thing is to develop the skills to identify and correct these negative mindsets. If we can learn to recognize cognitive distortions, then we'll have the ability to resist their harmful messages—and in doing this successfully over and over again, we can overcome them and adopt a more balanced and rational way of thinking. As with many skills in life, practice can make all the difference.

Negative thinking is part of the foundation of roadblocks, and it's crucial to avoid it whenever you can. Remaining positive will help you become more patient with yourself, and knowing that roadblocks will arise from time to time helps you remain positive.

You have little control over when and where challenging times will arise in your life, but you always have a choice about how you react. As difficult as it can be, you can choose to respond positively and find some good in those situations. There's always a productive takeaway. Never underestimate the power of optimism and positivity!

chapter eight

···

POSITIVE ADDICTIONS

Depending on what they are, our habits will either make us
or break us. We become what we repeatedly do.
—Sean Covey

Now that you've experienced this journey from negative addiction to connection, you might be wondering if there is such a thing as positive addiction. The answer is yes! Once we've transformed our thinking from self-limiting to limitless, creating positive addictions is the next logical step toward getting us where we want to go. Ultimately, we need to enlist the mind to help convince the body that we can interrupt old, soul-leaching habits and replace them with fresh, life-affirming ones. The good news is that you can reverse the negative momentum you may be dealing with to develop something that works on your behalf instead of against you.

William Glasser's 1976 book *Positive Addiction* focused mainly on the emotions underlying addictive behaviors. His notion of positive addiction can be defined as a healthy, habitual activity that enhances a person's life, reduces anxiety, and increases a sense of well-being. In short, it's something that routinely *makes you feel good*. It doesn't cause you to hide behind harmful behavior and instead invites you to be visible, confident, and in control.

Positive addiction promotes a sense of accomplishment in the specific activity and, more impressively, fosters a general feeling of wellness across all dimensions of life and relationships. This one small positive change can have a snowball effect, accumulating impact and becoming more and more beneficial to you. The rewards are long-term and can help encourage even more significant positive change to take root.

While a negative addiction detracts from personal strength in every part of life, a positive addiction should be pleasurable to carry out and offer the chance to experience strength, self-confidence, and an overall feeling of wellness. If the first step on the road to recovering from a negative addiction is recognition of the problem, then the first move toward a positive addiction should probably be acknowledgment of what type of beneficial activity you're seeking.

In his book, Glasser outlines six criteria that must be fulfilled in order to develop a positive addiction to an activity:[1]

1. It's noncompetitive.
2. It can be accomplished in approximately one hour a day.
3. It doesn't take a lot of effort.
4. It's of value to the person involved.
5. It's believed by the person that maintaining it will create improvement, but only that person gets to define *improvement*. Success is subjective.

6. Self-acceptance is part of the experience of carrying out the activity. Self-criticism has no place in it.

Following the above criteria will allow you to better choose and begin to embrace your positive addiction. To move out of negative addictions and into healthy, functional behaviors, it's also important to understand which of your needs you're trying to meet at any given time. So, how do you create a positive addiction that represents an amalgamation of your basic needs?

Keep in mind that balance is essential; after all, it's one of the basic needs that leads to success. Catering to one individual need over another can result in want or discontent. For example, if you overindulge security, you never get to have an adventure; and if you overdo adventure, you never get to have security. So, in a proportionate way, your positive addiction must address your basic needs for entertainment, connection, and spirituality. As you think about what your positive addiction will look like, consider the primary need it addresses.

While it seems easy to pick up and maintain harmful addictions, it may not seem as simple to establish positive addictions. This is in part because it's much easier to slip into the negative than it is to make a mindful decision that requires hard work and determination to succeed. So, when you weigh a positive addiction's possibility against the effort needed to develop it, you'll quickly realize that "easy" is relative. But don't be afraid of the formidable challenge; I suggest instead that you welcome it, because the benefits of greater inner peace, self-confidence, and well-being are at stake.

Good habits are worth being fanatical about.
~ John Irving

Choose Your Positive(s)

The choice of potential positive addictions is limitless, and for that reason, it may be challenging to figure out the best options. When making your selection, remind yourself that it needs to be beneficial for you either psychologically or physically, and perhaps both.

Why psychologically?

It may serve to soothe your mind and rest your soul. For example, a mental activity occupies time, allows for creativity, and calms the nerves.

Why physically?

It may increase physical health and feelings of well-being no matter your age, ability, or previous experience. Exercise provides focus and allows us to feel in control over at least one aspect of our existence.

Consider the whole picture, including your financial, physical, and scheduling parameters. Ask yourself how the activity will impact you and whether it will improve your life.

Can you envision a week in the future and predict how much more confident you will be? Are you willing to give it a chance?

If you put a little thought into identifying a few healthy behaviors, you'll find that it's not so difficult. Exercise, healthy eating, and sleep come immediately to mind, and are good places to start.

Positive Addictions to Inspire Your Thinking

—Running, walking, hiking, cycling, sailing

—Collecting stamps, coins, cards, or midcentury modern objects and furnishings

—Sewing, quilting, knitting, scrapbooking

—Gardening, bird-watching

—Listening to music, playing instruments, singing, dancing

—Drawing, painting, designing, reading, writing

—Learning languages, delving into history

—Eating healthfully, weight training

—Completing puzzles, playing chess

—Working in a food pantry, making blankets for those in shelters

—Acting, doing improv, stand-up comedy

—Practicing yoga or Tai Chi

—Meditating, engaging in mindfulness, exploring spirituality

Every time you are tempted to react in the same old way, ask if you want to be a prisoner of the past or a pioneer of the future.
~ Deepak Chopra

Although Glasser recommends devoting at least one hour a day to a positive addiction, the good news is that it can probably take as little as fifteen minutes when you start. You want your positive addiction to stay with you. It shouldn't dominate your life, but it should become an integral part of it—a practice that's carried out daily, almost without thought. The secret is to do it every day so that it becomes lodged in your procedural memory the way brushing your teeth, tying your shoelaces, and getting ready for work are. Once your chosen activity is easily accessible from your working memory, it will be automatic after thirty days.

Keep in mind that when learning a new task, multiple regions of the brain are activated, and this uses a great deal of energy. Once the task becomes a habit, however, less brain activity is needed to carry it out. This efficiency is our best friend when it comes to positive addiction and our focus on adaptive living.

The exciting new research on neuroplasticity and the ways in which the cells of the nervous system and the brain function together to mediate behavior is incredibly important. It can help us understand how parts of the brain are activated by addiction or withdrawal, and may ultimately provide helpful ideas for the treatment of negative addictions—and the promotion of positive ones. In short, if you change your behavior, you can change your addiction.

Assessing Readiness

Let's talk about the readiness state and the preparations you need to make to develop and experience your new positive habit.

Can you think of a time when you were willing and able to change, but it just didn't happen? Perhaps you weren't ready. The readiness state is based on the experiential realization that "of course I can!" and is the fuel that propels your ability and willingness into being. Readiness is being fully prepared and willing to do something. It suggests enthusiasm and optimism regarding the situation, goal, or procedure. We see readiness as the wellspring from which action that supports your positive addiction emerges. The more significant the change required, the more critical your awareness and understanding of your state of readiness is. This means having the right conditions and resources in place, having a definite and coherent vision of your objective, and having the correct mindset and perspective to create meaningful change.

In addition to readiness, the adoption and maintenance of your positive addiction are also predicated upon two additional traits:

1. Your *ability*, which refers to the extent to which you have the necessary skills, resources, and confidence to carry out the change.

2. Your *willingness*, which involves the importance placed on the actual change. For instance, how much is it needed or desired?

It is, of course, possible to have the ability to change but not the willingness to do so. Similarly, it's possible to be willing but lack the ability. Sometimes, even willingness and ability together aren't enough to instigate change. Again, readiness is what provides the necessary momentum. Determining your readiness state and then finding ways to expand it will provide the foundation for follow-through.

Questions to Help Identify Some
Right Positive Addictions

1. Am I interested in this?
2. Why is it vital for me to engage in this? (For example, "I want to look good"; "I want to think more clearly"; "I want to meet people.")
3. Is it essential for health reasons or because I simply want to feel better?
4. Am I choosing it because my friends do it, would be involved, want me to, keep bugging me about it and so forth?
5. Do I have what it takes (i.e., finances, physical ability, mental acuity)? What resources do I have that will help me achieve this goal?
6. How much time am I willing to devote to it daily?
7. How realistic am I being? What's the probability that there will be a payoff for my efforts, or that I'll be any good at it?
8. What are the logistics I have to consider?
9. Can I start immediately?
10. Can I stick with it?

A readiness state is one in which you take an inventory of the tools needed to accomplish a realistic task. According to Dar Gartrell, this is not a state of knowledge but a state of mind. You may access your readiness via social network, determination, skill sets, attributes, stick-to-it-ness, or other routes.

So, Are You Ready?

A necessary first step is an honest appraisal of what's required to engage in your chosen positive addiction, followed by an authentic evaluation of your ability to meet the requirements. Implementing change is a huge undertaking, and therefore readiness assessments can sometimes be referred to as "risk assessments." So, let's take a closer look at how to assess readiness, or implied risk, for the profound change your positive addiction is going to make in your life. It's important to determine whether you're ready or not and to be aware of everything we just talked about—hidden forces, overgeneralizations, and other things you might be doing that will stop you or inhibit success in the creation of a positive addiction.

Quiz: Ready or Not?
Answer the following questions with
yes, no, or sometimes.

1. When I run into trouble on a project or task, am I quick to look for a solution?
2. When confronted with difficulties, can I usually face things on my own?
3. Do I feel intimidated when beginning something new and challenging?
4. When starting a new project, do I break it down into manageable chunks?
5. Do I tend to get frustrated rather quickly when I try something unfamiliar?

6. Am I predictable and steady when it comes to maintaining a schedule?

7. If I don't like something, do I quickly move on to something else?

8. Do I have confidence in myself?

Answer Key: (1) Yes would be the best answer, suggesting you're ready to get started. (2) Again, yes is the best response, since you'll mostly be working on your positive addiction by yourself. (3) If you answered yes to this question, you may want to discuss your decision to create a positive addiction with a mentor before beginning. (4) Answering yes serves you well here. Baby steps are the best way to approach a positive addiction. (5) A yes answer indicates that you should take a closer look at your frustration tolerance and deal with that before embarking on the positive addiction. You need to give yourself some latitude for missteps and imperfection in order to succeed. (6) Saying yes to the capacity for keeping with a schedule is part of the bedrock of undertaking something new. You're ready to start your positive addiction. (7) If you answered yes to this question, take a little time to figure out how to stand by your choice. You need to be able to stick with your positive addiction until it becomes a habit, so trading it in for something else won't be helpful. (8) A yes here is a beautiful answer, of course. Keep in mind, however, that a sometimes or even a no can shift to a yes as you embrace your positive addiction. Note: Any sometimes responses might suggest that a bit more work is appropriate before moving ahead. Let this uncertainty act as gentle encouragement for additional proper preparation and not as reason to stop.

The length of time it can take to anchor a readiness state varies. Think about it in terms of one of our most strategic sports: before a golfer hits a ball, he or she takes several practice swings, focusing on where he or she wants the ball to go. These are fraction-of-a-second readiness states. A longer readiness state is in order when doing something such as packing for a trip, which involves a fair amount of forethought and action. And then there's the readiness state for a woman who's having a baby. In this case, the time required is forty weeks. By contrast, some people's occupations keep them in a constant and necessary state of readiness—for example, emergency response teams, firefighters, and police officers.

In each situation, there may be contextual, emotional, social, or psychological determinants in the mix. It may not be necessary to figure out what's behind your readiness state, but it's vital to determine just how ready you are before you begin.

From Idea to Application

Taking your positive addiction from the idea stage to the action stage can be challenging. You may find yourself caught in the default position of hesitation, procrastination, or fence-sitting, so let's take a closer look at what can help us make new and better decisions.

The first step is to act. It helps to frame your positive addiction as something you *get* to do, not something you *have* to do. For example, "I get to learn," "I get to walk with my friend," or "I get me time every day." We need to remind ourselves that language is powerful. "I get to do this" is the opposite of "I have to do this." Positive or negative, we listen to our self-talk, and the mind can't tell the difference between a real and an imagined thought. It believes what we tell it to.

An excellent way to start the process is by looking at the transactional analysis theory of personality and behavior. Formulated in 1961 by American psychiatrist Eric Berne, transactional analysis identifies the ego states behind all of life's transactions. In this instance, *ego* doesn't refer to self-importance but rather a state of being. Berne defined an ego state as "a consistent pattern of feeling and experience directly related to a corresponding consistent pattern of behavior."[3] He realized that within each of us exists a version of our parents, of ourselves as a child, and of us as an adult who has processed this information and applied it to our current life. This transactional analysis model can help illustrate how and why we may be experiencing difficulty connecting with our feelings and emotions in the first place, and, more important, what can help us as we move forward with a positive addiction.

Here's an outline of the three states:

PARENT EGO STATE

This represents the massive collection of recordings in the brain of the thoughts, behaviors, and feelings imposed on the child by the parents or parental figures in the environment in regard to external events experienced or perceived in the first five years of life. Everything the child observed their parents doing or saying is absorbed without question. Therefore, parental preferences, decisions, and prejudices are instilled in the child's belief system. This information can also be received

from older siblings, teachers, coaches, and other authority figures. This ego state contains many rules, usually applying to
how to behave, act, and feel.

Examples

"Never accept candy from strangers!"

"Be polite!"

"Always look both ways before you cross the street!"

Exercise

At some point in our lives, someone may have told us "You
sound like your mom" or "You sound like your dad." Can you
recall a time when you responded to a situation in the same
way one of your parental figures would? If you can, then you've
located your parent ego state.

CHILD EGO STATE

In contrast to the parent ego state, the child ego state represents
the recordings in the brain of internal reactions to external
events occurring during early childhood development, generally
before the age of five. Most of these early childhood experiences
are recorded as a spectrum of emotions, since the child doesn't
yet possess a developed vocabulary. The child in each of us is
often responsible for our creativity and sense of curiosity. Childhood emotions can resurface when a person is confronted with
different types of situations as they move into adulthood.

Examples

"When my mother threatened to leave the room, I always
felt scared."

"When it started to get dark at night, I got nervous."

"When I played in the water for the first time, I was happy."

Exercise

Consider how you responded to different situations as a child. How would you act when your parents chastised you for bad behavior? Would you express your anger about the situation by throwing a tantrum, or would you quietly sulk? Do you notice yourself acting similarly when faced with challenging circumstances today?

ADULT EGO STATE

This state is a direct response to the present in terms of attitudes, feelings, and behavior. It grows out of the child's ability to see the differences between what he or she *observed* from a parent and what he or she *felt*, and helps us to act accordingly in the here and now. The adult ego state allows the person to evaluate child and parental data and to process and validate information learned over time in order to change their thoughts, behaviors, and feelings in response to their current situation. An example would be your decision to comply with the COVID-19 restrictions in the interest of the greater good—i.e., to prevent the spread of the deadly virus. Your child ego state would want you to break the rules of lockdown and distancing in order to socialize with friends. Your parent ego state would say that it's important to follow rules. The adult ego state makes an informed decision.

Exercise

Think of a time when you confronted a situation and made a decision with an open mind and without prejudice. This response may be different from how the child in you would have dealt with it and how your parents would have reacted.

The three ego states can be summarized as follows:
Parent ego state refers to *taught* concepts.
Child ego state refers to *felt* concepts.
Adult ego state refers to *learned* concepts.

This is an adult ego state response. Instead of answering with the directives or orders of a parent ego state or the emotions of a child ego state, the adult ego state tends to lean toward logical problem solving.

Now that you understand these three ego states, you can achieve better insight into your actions and behavior in different situations. It isn't about one of them being right or wrong—it's about understanding all three and identifying how they contribute to your overall personality. If you continually pull out one of these ego states to present a facade to the world, you're going to have problems. However, by focusing on your reactions and feelings, you take steps to protect yourself from anxiety, addiction, and depression. You're also able to cope better through challenging periods in your life.

Try to come to an understanding of what your body, mind, and spirit are attempting to tell you from the perspective of all three ego states. As you go through life, you need to ensure that these three voices are working together. When you connect parental advice, child enthusiasm, and adult information, you can move forward congruently. It's a recipe for success!

Gwen represents an example of aligning the three voices. She was a forty-one-year-old social worker who was very attractive and sophisticated. She knew a great deal about nutrition, yet she kept gaining and losing weight. Gwen didn't seem to be able to stop herself from falling into this yo-yo cycle.

When we looked at her three ego states, we found that the parent voice was telling her, "You should eat clean." The child voice was saying, "No, I won't, and you can't make me." The adult voice was saying, "I should do this for my physical and mental health." Through the process of alignment, in which one becomes aware of one's ego states and the resulting behaviors (one of several forms of therapy that can apply here, as Ericksonian hypnosis could have worked well too), I got Gwen's child voice to say to her, "When I ate my greens at the dinner table, my mom smiled and my dad was happy. I felt happy." The parent voice said, "You should eat healthily," and the adult voice said, "I know what I have to do, and I now know I'm going to do it no matter what."

Gwen's adult ego state learned what it was that she needed to do differently. The child voice was throwing a temper tantrum and the parent voice was laying down rules; once she was able to align those two parts of her personality with her adult ego state, she was quite happy. She was able to maintain her weight loss for a considerable period of time, and reported increased energy and a feeling of contentment, which is something she hadn't felt for a long, long time.

Gwen told me, "I know I can do this because there's a gym close by. I know I can because I've got a plethora of information on nutrition. I know I can because my friends will support me. I know I can because I'm strong, tenacious, and determined."

chapter nine

....

MOTIVATION FOR
A HAPPIER LIFE

If you pick the right small behavior and sequence it right,
then you won't have to motivate yourself to have it grow. It will
just happen naturally, like a good seed planted in a good spot.
—B. J. FOGG

We've talked about positive addictions and the need for creating new, helpful habits as a stepping-stone to living a happier life. Your ability to be entranced, to be completely absorbed in today as it unfolds in a variety of small and significant ways, will help you to see, hear, feel, or even taste how your healthy habit can become an intrinsic part of you. The best positive addictions are maintained by energy, enthusiasm, and guarded optimism. The secret of their ultimate attainment lies not in your willpower but in your motivation.

We're all motivated by many circumstances and phenomena, including psychological factors such as urges, emotions, impulses, fears, wishes, pleasures, self-satisfaction, intrinsic satisfaction, likes, dislikes, goals, ambitions, values, mastery, and freedom. There are also physiological drives, such as survival and tangible rewards (money is a big one). So, what motivates some people to maintain positive addictions while others relapse into negative addictions? How many times have you not achieved something you wanted to achieve? Why didn't you achieve it? Was it because of a lack of resources, such as money or time?

No!

It was probably due to a lack of resourcefulness.

I have patients who tell me they've tried "it" (whatever that means) at least a hundred times. They typically say, "I tried everything, and then I gave up." Then I tell them, "Well, if you give up, it's never going to happen. You're never going to achieve that change."

I remember asking one of my patients, "When an infant becomes a toddler and tries to walk and falls down, do you chastise the child? Do you tell the child, 'You'd better give up'? Or are you endlessly patient and encourage the child to make the necessary changes to transition from crawling to standing up, and then from balancing to walking?" I don't think any parent would say that they berated their child for not being able to walk right away. And yet they often end up berating themselves when it comes to trying something new or doing something differently.

What about Thomas Edison and his development of the light bulb? Was it not one thousand times that he tried before he discovered a filament material that worked?

Joe had a gambling addiction. He insisted that he'd tried everything to quit, and nothing worked. He was a very successful businessman, but every so often he would disappear into a video lottery terminal and gamble his savings away. He would usually lose more than he would win. He kept it secret from his wife until she noticed that some bills weren't being paid and that their savings had disappeared. Soon they were in default because there was no positive cash flow.

Facing bankruptcy and the possible loss of his marriage, Joe finally accepted that he had to make some changes in his life. For starters, he decided to divorce himself from the addiction because he didn't want to divorce his wife. He knew that if he used that metaphor, it would help him disengage from something that was lethal to his marriage and to his self-esteem—not to mention his net worth.

The metaphor of a divorce—symbolically going to the courthouse and separating from the situation—helped Joe tremendously in ridding himself of the addiction. Moreover, whenever he felt the urge to gamble, he would send a note to his wife, letting her know how much he appreciated and loved her. She was impressed with the changes in Joe, but she took them with a bucketful of salt because she'd heard this before.

In a matter of five years, Joe moved from partial remission with a few slips to full remission. The gambling addiction was a thing of the past, but recovery was a difficult path for him because he was frustrated with himself. He felt that, as a perfectionist, he should have beaten this right away, and he didn't. He learned to accept the fact that the addiction was something over which he had no willpower, but that there were steps he could take to consciously break the pattern. Addition-ally, in a style of therapy developed by Milton Erickson, an ordeal was thrown into the process as well: if Joe decided to gamble, he had to give the same amount of money he lost to an organization that he despised. By doing this, and enlisting his wife's support, he was able to control the urge and to break the addiction, not just the habit.

Why is it so hard to do the little things that will improve our life?

Whenever we hesitate, this micro-movement sends a signal to the brain. This interaction is called the "spotlight effect." It's the brain's way of protecting us from doing some-thing that frightens us or that can cause potential harm. Renowned author and motivational speaker Mel Robbins developed a way to stop us from hesitating when we're faced with something we *know* we should do, however scary it may seem. Her advice is to count out five seconds—five, four, three, two, one—to activate your prefrontal cortex and interrupt the habit of overthinking, self-doubt, and fear. Robbins recog-nizes that the motivation to go after your goals, big or small, doesn't come instantly to you, nor does it stay. That's why her 5 Second Rule is vital for helping push you to accomplish your goal(s). It's all about taking action. Robbins has found that the moment you have an instinct to act on a goal, you must physically move within five seconds or your brain will stop you.[1] This rule utilizes a form of metacognition, or a method of tricking your brain so you can succeed in your goals. It breaks our pattern of living on autopilot! It acknowledges that many of us have some habits that don't increase the quality of our lives. All too often we default to what seems safe and easy, and then we feel out of control because of this default method of living. It's especially uplifting during difficult times to know that we can have control over our actions and their outcomes, and that in turn, we can achieve our goals.

Of course, so much stress in life is caused by not finishing what we start. We've all been there. And when our to-do list starts looking like a twenty-car pileup, it's hard to get out from under it. There end up being many things we don't complete, ranging from household tasks and courses that earn us an educational degree or a driver's license to plans for backing out of a marriage. Big or small, incompletions can lead to a sense of inadequacy, deficiency, failure, lack of focus, and, ultimately, unhappiness. It's neither possible nor appropriate to follow through on every invitation, of course, but there are certain ones whose benefits are more than worth the effort. The pursuit of your positive addiction is one of those.

Are you motivated to change—and will your positive addiction support your motivation?

Select an activity that seems promising, and over time, what was promising can become fulfilling.

Here's a quick self-check inspired by achievement needs and some common motivators we've identified thus far. Think honestly about yourself and note which of the following you respond to most readily.

1. Approval of others.
2. Monetary reward.
3. Personal gratification for a job well done.
4. Reduced stress in life.
5. Avoidance of failure at all costs.
6. Opportunities to excel physically, mentally, spiritually, emotionally, and intellectually.
7. Team-oriented activities.
8. Immediate gratification.
9. Public recognition (or, conversely, a need for privacy).
10. Connecting with others.

There may be other motivators not mentioned in this list, so feel free to add your own. Identifying personal motivators will help you customize your pursuit of positive addictions with appropriate reinforcements. For instance, if winning the approval of others is what makes you tick, then find a way to incorporate this motivator into your positive addiction. If you're having a hard time getting started, ask a person you admire to mentor you. Perhaps this individual would be willing to talk with you once a week and offer encouraging observations about your success, or possibly to text you at specified times with notes of inspiration, or even to leave short, mood-bolstering messages on your voice mail a couple of times a week.

Tips for Strengthening and Maintaining Motivation

There are many things you can do to increase your resolve. The following are my top ten suggestions.

1. Start with baby steps.
2. Visualize your goals (e.g., by leaving pictures or quotes on the fridge).
3. Use a buddy system.
4. Exercise patience.
5. Chart your progress.
6. Self-reinforce regularly.
7. Know why you're doing something (e.g., create checklists).
8. Think positively.
9. Focus on the gain, not the loss, but never skip two days in a row. (Even when circumstances make it necessary to make an adjustment, carry out your commitment.)
10. Preplan and use positive self-talk such as "I get to start," "I will take the first step," or "I choose to . . ."

No matter which one you choose, once you select your positive addiction and get started, you can expect to begin getting unstuck from the quagmire of self-doubt, unhappiness, and feelings of underachieving.

While I always encourage connection, some people are probably better off choosing a positive addiction they can take part in alone. These people tend to avoid being in positions where they might receive negative reinforcement from others or where they might constantly seek praise. This can be uncomfortable for them and perhaps set up a roadblock. There will be many distractions that vie for your time and focus, and by avoiding any potential roadblocks you may find it less challenging to keep at it.

If you do start off solo, you'll eventually want to include others in your goal action plan—not for their approval but for their support. For example, if your objective is clean eating and you're enjoying the new recipes you're preparing, share them with others and invite them to share their healthy recipes with you too. At the end of the day, is there anything more important than feeling better, getting stronger, being happier, and having a more fulfilling life?

Motivation involves the ability to be aware of personal goals, to recognize discrepancies between current behaviors and desired ideals, and to resolve ambivalence about making positive changes.[2] It serves as that extra push you give yourself when you feel like quitting. Its basis is the desire to see or make changes, and it's a crucial element in setting goals and being able to work toward completion.

People often say that motivation doesn't last. Well, neither does bathing—that's why we recommend it daily.
— Zig Ziglar

Identifying Your Personal Motivation Pathway

Psychologist Martin Seligman said, "Authentic happiness comes from identifying and cultivating your most fundamental strengths and using them every day in work, love, play, and parenting."[3] So, when you're thinking of developing a positive habit, consider matching your character strengths to the challenges of life. What's your style? How do you approach life? What's your natural preference for being?

Now that we've identified what we know (or don't know) about motivation, let's tie it to personal life pathways, or the unique styles, approaches, and preferences each one of us uses to connect with life in general.

Try to identify with one or more of the following pathways. Several may have relevance, but one or two will likely resonate more than the others. Recognition of which ones draw you more than others will assist with motivation for your positive addiction. In my practice, I've found that people often choose different combinations. Which combination do you want? There are many different ways that people interact with their environment and with themselves; the following examples are presented in order to help you sort out which approaches are right for you.

CEREBRAL PATHWAY

Those who adopt this pathway are drawn to learning and intellectual pursuits. They prefer using their heads to using their hearts. They're scholars and thinkers who are inspired by new data.

Effect on Motivation: If you've chosen a positive addiction outside of intellectual pursuits—i.e., you've taken up something more physical, such as tennis—be sure to include rewards within the cerebral realm for when you finish your lesson or match. Take time out to read news articles or do innovative research. This balance will increase your stick-to-it-ness. Know which specific intellectual pursuits engage you. Make a list of activities (solving brain teasers, for example) that will serve as instant reinforcement and reward for the small successes you have on the court.

Robert, a university professor in his early forties, wanted to engage in a positive addiction. He set out to do something more sports-oriented. He started running, but soon lost momentum. He tried outdoor cycling on a road bike, but didn't find it to be sustainable either, as he had difficulty doing it on a regular basis.

As we explored options together, it became apparent that a better choice might have been something related to philosophy. Robert was very interested in existentialism, and this matched his cerebral pathway. He was very excited about this journey, since he had never really had time to examine the subject in depth. He reported being able to follow through on this option far better than he could on the others. To create balance in his life, he linked this new positive addiction with a physical activity: he decided to walk to campus each day instead of driving. This fifteen-minute trek afforded him some physical activity as well as additional time to think. Later, he joined an online chess club and increased his circle of friends.

INTROSPECTIVE PATHWAY

To people on this pathway, reflection and meditation come easily. They prefer to be alone, and may even have difficulty interacting with others.

Effect on Motivation: Understand that if you fall in this category but choose a pursuit from outside this realm, your rewards should include some alone time, as that's what's motivating to you. If you want to challenge yourself, try choosing a positive addiction that involves relationships, but be aware of the connection difficulties that might emerge.

Isabella was a very introverted, self-conscious person who constantly worried about what people might be thinking of her, which made her self-critical and affected her self-esteem. One of the positive addictions Isabella chose was learning to play bridge, which enabled her to meet two goals at the same time: she was able to interact with other people and form some new relationships, and she enjoyed the "mental gymnastics" that the game demanded. She has continued with this positive addiction for the past few years. When last I spoke to her, she was thinking of starting a bridge club at her home.

OUTDOORSY PATHWAY

Nothing is better than being in nature for these people. They'll do whatever is necessary to escape from the indoors. They may have difficulty sitting at a desk for an extended period, for example. Often, they prefer being alone with nature over sharing it with others.

Effect on Motivation: If your chosen positive addiction must be carried out inside, try to find ways to include nature.

An activity such as watching a nature video while running on a treadmill might work. Reward yourself by setting aside special outdoors time when you've accomplished what you set out to do. At the end of a good workout, for example, you might take a brisk walk no matter the weather conditions. Or go full blue and green and select a positive addiction that's set in the outdoors. You'll get a bigger bang for your buck.

Roger loved being outdoors. There was nothing that he enjoyed more than communing with nature. He felt more at peace and more connected when he was in the mountains. For him, being there was easy. He experienced flow. Roger's most important epiphany was realizing that he needed to do more of what was natural and easy for him—things that involved some planning but not a lot of self-discipline. He recounted how time stood still when he lost his way once during a hike in the Rocky Mountains. He enjoyed each rock as he climbed upward, stopping occasionally to take in the scenery. This allayed his anxiety about being lost, allowing him to get his bearings and be calmed by the beauty of his surroundings. For Roger, being in nature and having time for contemplation on his own were very important. He ultimately combined these needs with positive addictions to fly-fishing, trail-bike riding, and more hiking. Once he engaged in these activities routinely, Roger reported feelings of inner peace, tranquility, calm, and increased connection with himself and others. They were also wonderful ways for him to practice problem solving on his own.

SERVICE PATHWAY

People on this pathway are the "servers" of humankind. They get joy and fulfillment from giving to and helping others. They may have difficulty, however, being the recipients of gifts, gratitude, and affection in return.

Effect on Motivation: As reinforcement for positive addiction successes outside the service realm, allow yourself time to help someone you've wanted to connect with but haven't necessarily had the time to do so, no matter how small the gesture may seem. You might call or e-mail an old friend or drop a card to someone who's been having challenges.

Plan your positive addiction so that you can perform it alone and thus not be in the position of having to regularly receive positive reinforcement from others, as this will be uncomfortable for you and perhaps create obstacles along the way.

When I first met Andrew, he was a thirty-five-year-old Anglican minister. He reported feelings of inadequacy that would arise whenever he had to deliver a sermon. This was his first parish, and, arguably, his relative lack of experience triggered these feelings. One of the ways he overcame his shyness and self-consciousness was to focus on his new congregation. His positive addiction included reaching out and talking with parishioners on a one-to-one basis during the week. In doing this, Andrew was able to weave some of the content of his upcoming homily into his conversations—not the whole thing, of course, but a theme or two that applied to what the parishioner was experiencing at the time. These conversations focused on things like bereavement, financial difficulties, loss of a relationship, overall sadness, or being shut in. In having these discussions, Andrew was able to use his positive addiction to help overcome his self-consciousness.

By connecting individually with his parishioners, Andrew experienced an incredible sense of peace while also doing something that was constructive and of service. How did this translate into his homilies? In the past, he would have anxiety attacks on Sundays. Now, however, he could look forward to delivering his sermon by imagining that he was having an intimate conversation with each of his parishioners.

KINSHIP PATHWAY

People who are kinship-oriented love relationships. They enjoy being with others and require close connection. They thrive on having company, and their significant relationships are essential.

Effect on Motivation: If you're on this pathway, be sure to create a list of reinforcement activities that includes others.

Marlene was a thirty-six-year-old hairstylist who was both a wife and a mother. She wanted to read more but couldn't find the time or the motivation to pursue this task on her own. She joined an online book club and found that the structure helped her to complete a novel each month. It also gave her the opportunity to connect with others. She'd tried several clubs in the past to no avail, but this particular club was full of like-minded women in her age group who were going through similar experiences and facing similar issues. She felt connected, supported, and able to contribute.

PROPELLING PATHWAY

These are action-oriented people who hate sitting still and are always on the go. They get joy from activity and possess a passion for challenges. They're determined, and are frequently in pursuit of a cause.

Effect on Motivation: If the chosen positive addiction in any way limits physical activity and invites slowing down (such as writing poetry or learning a new language), plan for shorter spans of that activity, coupled with intermittent bursts of more energetic undertakings. For example, after studying Spanish for a certain amount of time, take a break to run on the treadmill for five minutes before continuing. Create a list of quick reinforcements so that when you hit a roadblock, there's an activity waiting for you. Can't sit still to write? Do sixteen jumping jacks and then try again.

Alan, a firefighter, came to me to discuss the possibility that he had attention deficit disorder with hyperactivity. His wife complained that he would start tasks and not complete them. He meant well, but their basement, for example, was in constant disarray. I could empathize with his wife for loving him and wanting to strangle him at the same time. He could deliver a cogent argument for why he was doing what he was doing, but nothing was ever completed. For instance, he started fixing the bathroom but suddenly switched gears and went into the garage to sort tools. While doing this, he decided that he should install a new garage-door opener. Of course, this left the family without a garage door for months.

Alan's wife had called me and asked if I would consult with him, since she was at her wit's end about what to do. After I'd worked with Alan for a while, he was able to set himself up with a timeline that allowed him to stop whatever he was doing for approximately ten minutes and engage in another activity. These structured diversions assured that he was able to complete his primary tasks in a timely fashion—usually within six months, as compared to three or four years of total chaos. Since Alan enjoyed playing games on the computer, he decided that he would work for longer intervals and then take ten-minute time-outs to play computer games. After these time-outs, he would continue with the main task. He varied his reinforcements so that during the next break, he would go for a walk or a bike ride with his son, which was something that he really enjoyed doing. Eleven year-old Ethan loved spending time with his dad.

Once Alan was able to create a schedule with a good task-to-break ratio and enough variation in his breaks, he reported feelings of satisfaction—and his wife felt relieved because things were actually being done and the chaos had, to a certain extent, subsided. Alan was able to apply this system in other areas of his life as well, setting diversions every sixty minutes. He utilized his strengths and the knowledge that he needed to be on the go in a way that was productive. You could say that he learned to put out fires at home.

PRODUCTIVE PATHWAY

The people who take this approach to life are designers, creators, and pursuers of the fine arts. They include people such as builders, architects, and inventors. They want to know how things are put together. These people are good with their hands and experience great joy in creation.

Effect on Motivation: Activities that are repetitive and don't enlist the imagination may be very tough. This doesn't mean that physical activities such as running shouldn't be considered; it simply means that the person must be aware of what fuels their creativity.

This reminds me of Angela. She always dressed impeccably, regardless of the season. She was thirty-two years old, had bachelor's and master's degrees in fine arts, and was starting to develop her own brand of clothing. Angela had gone to trade shows and been very successful, and was publicized in local newspapers. While she could pursue these creative outlets and derive a lot of satisfaction, her challenge was that she was unable to meet her financial commitments due to a downturn in the economy. She'd thought of going back into teaching, but she hated the routine. She liked to do things outside of the box.

In the wee hours of the morning, Angela would have flashes of inspiration for her next creations, be they leather handbags, hats, or other accessories. One of the things Angela decided to do was to connect with other women who were successful in different areas, and to ask one in particular, a woman named Mary-Lynne, whether she would be interested in becoming a silent partner in her company. After much negotiation, Mary-Lynne came on board. This relieved some of Angela's financial stress and afforded her the opportunity to continue her creative work. For her, it was important to be able to work with leather, her hands, and her imagination to create beauty out of nothing. Angela's work was her avocation, and she was passionate about it. Time would stand still when she was creating; she was in flow, and it would be agonizing whenever inspiration was lacking.

In general, being aware of your motivational pathways can help with the planning of not only your proactive emergency activities but also your daily "work toward the goal" actions. Always remember to respect your individual style. Tailor your approach to developing a positive addiction to what you already value. Go slowly and be artistic or logical, if that's your style. If you're emotional, find a way to use your emotions to your benefit. By honoring your individuality instead of trying to adapt to a "perfect style," you'll build confidence and achieve higher self-esteem.

Sometimes Life Gets in the Way

Unfortunately, motivation is often stimulated and sometimes thwarted by life-altering events that are completely beyond our personal control. For example, the sudden death of a family member or close friend may lead us to think about either making drastic life changes for the better or giving up. While the initial situations may be out of our hands, how we respond to them is not.

Distress levels: If distress levels are unusually high, they can motivate change or get in the way of change.

Critical life events: Certain life events stand out as prompts to embrace change. Such events include being in a life-threatening accident, suffering a severe illness, the death of a loved one, becoming pregnant or not being able to get pregnant, getting married, or getting divorced.[4] Serious circumstances such as these can lead to cognitive evaluation or appraisal in which the individual is forced to consider the impact of the event. In the aftermath, they may feel compelled to fall back on negative addictions. Particularly challenging circumstances can dramatically decrease motivation and get in the way of necessary change. The affected person may feel that life no longer means what it did before the event, and thus they no longer have a strong motivation for change.

Recognition of negative consequences of actions: The acknowledgment of the negative consequences of an action or actions and the harm or hurt that has been inflicted on others or oneself motivates some people to change.[5]

External incentives: Both positive and negative external incentives can influence motivation. Supportive friends, rewards, and positive (and negative) feedback can all stimulate motivation to make positive or negative changes.

Fatigue and time constraints: Both can have adverse effects on the motivation for working toward a positive addiction goal.

Any of these variables can be considered red flags, as they interfere with motivation. As we've said, preparation is the linchpin of any plan. Feeling ambushed by challenges puts us at a disadvantage just when we need to be proactive and flexible enough to deal with them.

No matter how strong our desire to change may be, it's not enough on its own. Personal change requires know-how (learning) as well as desire (motivation). To grow and develop new habits and positive addictions, knowledge is necessary—but in terms of just how much progress is accomplished, motivation is the key.

For example, we may know how to read, but we won't be able to find out what happens at the end of the story unless we're motivated to finish it. Change comes about when know-how and desire work together. That's how this book came about!

There will undoubtedly be occasions when our desire is just not strong enough for us to invest the necessary time and effort to make our goals a reality. Change cannot occur when a lack of motivation interferes with the required action. Sometimes we fool ourselves into thinking that we can reach our objective quickly and easily with little or no effort, but real change doesn't happen that way. Without a doubt, you're going to have to work for it.

Setting Goals

When patients come to see me, I prompt them to talk about their problem. My orientation is to establish the endpoint first: What is the ultimate goal? How can we achieve that according to ego state? In chapter eight, I talked about the parent, adult, and child voices; all three ego states must be in alignment so you don't have the rebellious child voice saying, "I won't do it if I'm being made to, even if I want to." What you want is to get to a place where you, as an adult, say to your child voice, "I will because I want to, no matter who [myself or anybody else] says I have to." Owning the result no matter what is the critical issue here.

So, participate in your positive addiction because you want to. I don't say to myself, "I *should* read journals for five hours a week" or, "I've *got* to read journals"; I change it to, "I *get* to read journals for five hours a week." Something as simple as changing the vowel in one word from *o* to *e* in the above statements makes an experiential shift possible.

Whatever harmful habit you may be looking to rid yourself of, you can first decide on a goal and then understand that the readiness state required to reach that goal is also a transitional state. The contemplation of your positive addiction starts with motivation and readiness, followed by a decision to act and then follow-through. Deciding to act is an important step that can empower you to become self-determined and to reframe your situation. It instills within you the feeling that you are the architect of your own life and can make changes for the best.

An understanding of the psychological model will help reinforce your ability to deal with whatever difficulties come up as you pursue your desired goals. Setting specific objectives, being able to identify them clearly, and figuring out what will be required to achieve them are keys to improving your well-being. Understandably, people who attain many or most of their goals are usually calmer and happier, and report feeling in control of their lives.

It may be beneficial to try to think of your positive addiction as both a goal and a pathway. Both short- and long-term goals have places in the realization of change. Goals need to be broken down into small steps if we are to reach them. For example, you may set a goal for yourself to become stronger and healthier by engaging in routine exercise. Exercise is not only a short-term goal but also a way to achieve your overall intention of improved health, which is a long-term payoff.

Helpful Approaches to Goal Setting

When it comes to goal setting, remember that what works for one person doesn't necessarily work for another. By understanding different approaches, you can mix and match strategies, and even come up with new ones if necessary.

Here are a few suggestions for engaging in your positive addictions:

THE POSITIVE APPROACH

When identifying specific components of the goal, remember that positive objectives are more motivating than negative ones. "I choose to develop increased body strength and plan to start with small steps" is more motivating than, "I'd like to be less nervous about not meeting my goal." This approach will serve you well as you start your positive addiction—and when you hit the inevitable roadblocks along the way.

It might also be valuable to create a list of favorite motivational quotes that you can place in a highly visible location so you're routinely reminded of their uplifting message. For example, a woman I knew who was going through chemotherapy wrote down inspirational sayings that she posted on the mirror in her bathroom so she could see them several times a day. Some posts were about staying strong, while others were goals she had for when she finally "kicked cancer's ass." These daily reminders helped her stay strong throughout her battle.

When I was in my twenties, the cool thing to do was to smoke. In order to fit in, I picked up the habit. As I recall, I was into the menthol variety of the brand Craven A. It kept me cool, if you'll pardon the pun! My Swedish friend Lilian, whom I hadn't seen for years, bumped into me one day and was shocked to see me smoke. I told all my friends, "It's the menthol that I'm hooked on." But this was really just an elegant way of practicing denial. Of course I was hooked on the nicotine. Whenever I felt stressed, I'd think, "Wouldn't it be nice to have a Craven A?" And then I would light up, take a few puffs, and put out the cigarette.

I went to Europe, and in Paris, much to my surprise, they didn't have the Craven A brand. There was a wide variety of different mentholated cigarettes, but none of them was just right. That's when I pondered quitting, but that didn't last very long. As soon as I got back to Canada, I renewed my friendship with Craven A menthols. I realized that telling people I was going to quit and then breaking my promise created a lot of havoc. I felt badly about having let down people who cared about me, and awful about displaying such an abysmal lack of willpower.

When I looked at nicotine from the point of view of choice, I was able to choose freedom. I chose not to let any substance control me. I opted to do this for my body and, since I was an avid runner, to increase my speed and stamina. This was a positive approach for me in which I called the shots, including allowing myself to have some relapses if necessary. I said to myself, "If I choose today and it doesn't work—if *today* I light up—I can always count on tomorrow to be a better day." With this approach, I was able to see myself doing things differently. I was able to break the pattern of having a cigarette with my morning coffee. I broke the need for it as a stress release, choosing to listen to music instead.

It took me approximately one month to break the habit and five more years before I felt I was really free of it, because unlike a lot of ex-smokers, when I would smell smoke on other people I would inhale it, enjoying the secondary smoke. After those five long years, I was finally out of that phase, too, and had developed a new sensitivity to people with addictions. I knew from personal experience that it's not easy and that quitting has nothing to do with willpower. Rather, it had everything to do with the image that I held in my mind and the carrot of freedom that I dangled in front of myself. As a bonus, my running speed increased, as did my respect for my body.

THE PERSONAL ORIENTATION

Another point to consider when specifying your goal is your orientation. Performance-oriented people view learning as something beyond their control. They're more likely to strive for outside attention and to see failure as an inability to be successful, not something one can recover from. They tend to be extrinsically motivated and exhibit weaker self-regulatory patterns.

Mastery-oriented people realize success depends on the skill set brought to bear. They tend to work harder than performance-oriented people because they believe it's possible to learn. They also tend to be self-directed and to achieve a higher level of goal attainment.

When faced with a roadblock, a performance-oriented person might give up quickly because of feelings of inadequacy. A mastery-oriented person is more likely to demonstrate increased practice and effort in response to the same barrier.

Understanding your personal orientation can help you meet your goal through smaller, more achievable components. For example, if you know you're performance-oriented, plan for constructive management of whatever might get in your way instead of waiting until disruptions occur and being troubled by the feelings that are ignited by them. Knowing that you've planned for complications will allow you to respond and overcome obstacles effectively. Which are you? Performance-oriented or mastery-oriented? Or a combination of both?

TASK-FOCUSED MOTIVATION

To be successful in creating positive addictions, your motivation needs to be focused on essential tasks that will help you get there. Much time is wasted doing things that are unimportant instead of spotlighting what's necessary and appropriate. Efficiency is greatly increased when you focus on the important aspects of what you do. Your positive addiction will require a time commitment, but in return you'll gain access to your best self.

ACHIEVABLE GOALS

Challenging but attainable goals are themselves motivating. If a goal is too simple, it becomes uninspiring and boring, which causes motivation to quickly drop off. On the other hand, impossible goals are frustrating, too, and motivation slips away in response. We're most motivated when we feel capable, responsible, stimulated, and hopeful. So, when preparing to begin your positive addiction, check your ultimate goal as well as your smaller, step-by-step goals, and be sure they're reasonable but challenging.

In summary, to get where you want to go, you'll first need to have a well-formed vision of the endpoint of the process. Focus on the solution. It's vital to get into a readiness state by reminding yourself of the privilege in front of you. Say things such as, "I can because I want to," "I get to do this," or "I get to do this for me."

So what happened to the seven-year-old girl who felt so lonely and disconnected at boarding school? Her vulnerability is still present. At times it's as if she suddenly realizes she's naked in a public place. Cowriting *The Habit of a Happy*

Life with Dr. Jeffrey Zeig was easier for me than writing this book solo. I still get butterflies in my stomach before I give a talk. It's like training for a marathon—sleep, nutrition, practice, and a whole heap of "stick-with-it-ness" is required. The little girl learned about the power of time affluence and about the power of buying things that last in memory only, such as vacations, concerts, and experiences shared with someone else. Early on, her prefrontal cortex would routinely miscalculate how much pleasure or dissatisfaction an item or an event would cause. She would purchase an object, grow used to it, then lose interest in it. Now she monitors her miswanting and misspending[6]—not that she doesn't have occasional lapses. Her experience simulator can do with frequent tune-ups! I recall my accountant telling me, "If you're not happy with what you're buying, you're misspending." He was referring to stocks, but I was never meant to be a farmer, so why should I put stock in sacred cows? I gleefully told him that I had spent money on a scholarship for a Thai graduate student instead. "Well," he said, "I hope the scholarship has a tax credit to it." "No," I said, "it's not a registered charity, and I'm ecstatic about my investment." I trusted Boonsri, my Thai friend with whom I completed graduate studies, to select the right student. My accountant turned a deep shade of red. I think it would be fair to say he wasn't happy with me.

We tend to revert to our level of life satisfaction a year after good or bad events have occurred in our lives. That's impact bias for you! According to Dan Gilbert, there exists "the tendency for the simulator to work badly . . . to make you believe that different outcomes are more different than in fact they really are."[7] Haven't you noticed how easy it is for you to convert a potentially bad situation into one that's more palatable? That's our psychological immune system at work. News flash: happiness can be manufactured! Lyubomirsky points out that 40 percent of our happiness comes from how we process situations and events.[8]

In my twenties I was involved in a near-fatal motor-vehicle accident. Recovery was long and difficult. I would often go down the rabbit hole of asking "Why me?" until I realized that the question "Why not me?" was the key to my moving forward. My psychological immune system kicked in. I learned that I could control my thoughts. I looked at my circustances as an opportunity to build relationships with those around me who were being supportive. My new interpretation of the accident was necessary to my happiness. Research tells us that only 10 percent of happiness comes from life events.[9] DNA can claim only 50 percent responsibility. Think about that! Experiences and genetics are only part of the equation; our *perceptions* of our experiences are what really create happiness. In winter, would you ever put on your coat first, followed by your pants, shirt, underpants, boots, and socks? That's a crazy thought, huh? But happiness isn't contingent on the order of events in your life. You can manufacture happiness before, during, or after any major life event. Happiness is not an act; it's a *habit*. Maintaining love, laughter, connection, gratitude, volunteerism, mindfulness, healthy choices, and the re-creation of our village are some of the ways to open the door to happiness. What are the keys that could unlock your happiness? How do you regulate your negative thoughts? Could you be happier than you currently are? If so, imagine those choices and incorporate them into your life one by one. Happiness really does await you.

chapter ten

BECOMING AN INGENIOUS SURVIVOR DURING DYSTOPIAN TIMES
THE COVID-19 CRISIS AND BEYOND

If you treat an individual as he is, he will remain how he is.
But if you treat him as if he were what he ought to be and could be,
he will become what he ought to be and could be.
—JOHANN WOLFGANG VON GOETHE[1]

A significant portion of this book addresses the subject of loneliness and its effect on happiness. It has always been a timely subject, but never more so than now. In December of 2019 the novel coronavirus that causes COVID-19 was detected in Wuhan, China, in a possible zoonotic jump from pangolins to humans. As of this writing, the original transmission of the virus is still unconfirmed. What we do know, of course, is that COVID-19 affects our respiratory system. It also affects our vascular system. It has impacted a high percentage of our population. By March of 2020, what started as an epidemic had quickly become a global pandemic, affecting the very fabric of our society. The meaning of happiness has become skewed. The authors of the World Happiness Report argue that maintaining social contact, albeit at a distance, is crucial for our happiness.[2] Distance socializing has since become the norm in our everyday lives.

In an attempt to stop the rapid spread of the virus, we have been asked to stay at home, to self-isolate, to self-quarantine, and to practice social distancing of at least six feet (or two meters) when necessity brings us out into public spaces.

On March 20, 2020, the World Health Organization (WHO) amended these guidelines to correct the terminology being used. In recognition of the importance of human connection, the WHO replaced the term *social distancing* with the more apt *physical distancing*. The latter reminds us that while we need to leave safe physical space between us in order to reduce the potential for the transmission of the virus, there is still a need for social interaction, if only through such connections as telephone calls, Skype, Zoom, Snapchat, and FaceTime. The change in language acknowledges the importance of also maintaining our mental health as we strive to sustain our bodily health. But here's the twist: while we used to leave our homes to socialize, now we must spend vast amounts of time within our homes as part of practicing distant socializing!

What follows is a perspective on how to cope with the many unknowns of the pandemic, the various safety measures we've adopted, the complexity of emotions we feel in this era (now being referred to as the "Great Adaptation"), and their impact on our sense of happiness. Though this chapter has been written with the events surrounding COVID-19 in mind, the underlying principles apply in all times of public health crisis and in situations of high anxiety.

Early Stages

Self-isolation and self-quarantine, of course, can have deleterious effects, causing people to feel entrapped, to experience a loss of connection, and to become anxious or depressed. This affects people of all age groups, but it's particularly difficult for senior citizens, those who live alone, people whose immune systems are compromised, and nursing-home patients. Those suffering from dementia cannot self-regulate, so they're often unaware of subjective symptoms, including those that are flu-like. Checking in by phone with people in these vulnerable groups is vital to maintaining their spirits, as well as monitoring their physical well-being.

The psychological impact of states of emergency and of home confinement can raise our levels of anxiety, stress, and fear. In these times, the routines that ground us tend to be discontinued. People with preexisting mental conditions are at risk of having their symptoms exacerbated. Social isolation implies the absence of social contact. Self-quarantine can be interpreted as being under house arrest. It's up to us to attune to others' needs, to offer help and support when necessary, and to normalize the situation whenever possible. One small way to do this is by making appropriate eye contact and extending a verbal greeting such as, "Continue to be safe" or, "Enjoy your walk" to those you pass on the street or to the essential workers keeping our daily needs met—all while maintaining the requisite six-foot distance, of course. I also recommend chatting across the fence with a neighbor. Smiles—even under masks—can be sensed and are contagious in the best of ways. They infect us with joy.

In such trying times, loneliness is not the only feeling we'll experience. Anxiety is prevalent too. Note, however, that it's not a bad thing to experience a little anxiety. That initial constriction in the chest serves to protect us in the face of a perceived threat. It's natural to feel it as you sanitize commonly used items such as light switches, door handles, toilet handles, cell phones and other devices, or when you shop for groceries at your local store and acknowledge that it's no longer a place to linger or socialize. Maintaining distance, lining up to enter, touching only the items you wish to purchase, and leaving while still maintaining physical distance can make a place that once felt very comfortable feel quite alienating now. Seeing empty shelves or low quantities of items you usually consume can cause stress, as can worries about the cleanliness of grocery carts or the handles on freezer-section doors. You question whether it's safe to pick up a can or goods packaged in cardboard. You may wonder if someone else picked it up before you. Are there asymptomatic carriers shedding coronavirus around you? When you're struck by such fears, try to think of them as questions whose answers will ultimately guide you. There's a difference between *knowing* the rules of protecting yourself and *understanding* them. Understanding creates mindful compliance with those rules, and can go a long way toward reducing your anxiety. For instance, you may know that it's generally wise to maintain clean hands, but once you understand that washing with soap and water for twenty seconds dissolves the lipid surface of COVID-19 viruses, you're more likely to maintain the habit of keeping those hands spotless. By understanding the facts, you can actually help regulate your anxiety. The same is true for wearing a mask in public: it serves to prevent you from unwittingly spreading the virus if you're an asymptomatic carrier. It reduces the anxiety of those around you, too, particularly those who are vulnerable because they're in high-risk groups.

Why is this event causing more hypervigilance and anxiety than any we've collectively faced before? Well, unless you're eighty years old, I'm guessing you haven't experienced anything as major in your lifetime. The Spanish flu pandemic of 1918 and both world wars likely predated you and are known to you only through what you've read in history books, seen in movies, or heard from your parents or grandparents. This pandemic is not unlike one of those wars, but this time the conflict is with a hidden enemy. The good news—which ought to stem some of your anxiety—is that people can unite to fight against this enemy instead of turning on one another, as we unfortunately did in prior wars. Our life expectancy was also much shorter all those years ago—and we didn't have the kind of real-time global news coverage we have today. The added perspectives both of these factors lend us at this time are very useful. To be sure to keep these advantages from becoming disadvantages, however, we have to be able to distinguish between viable information and *mis*information. Since our cognitive biases lead us to agree with issues that fit with our mindset, it's important to limit our media consumption as much as possible to reliable sources. Doing so will help reduce stress. The sheer volume of media alone can fuel anxiety, so also be mindful of the number of hours you spend catching up on the news, as well as the origin of the content.

Even when the intel we're getting makes sense, there's an understandable element of doubt. We can engage in behaviors such as washing our hands with soap, disinfecting surfaces, physical distancing, self-isolating, self-quarantining, and wearing masks when in public, but something inside us is aware that until we've discovered how to overcome this virus, we can't know for sure what will happen next. In the Greek language, *chaos* means a gaping void or emptiness that existed before things came into being. To cope with the unknown and mitigate our anxiety, we can choose to fill the void of social interaction—aka the "chaos" that void creates—with self-care. Be mindful of your emotions and thoughts without judging them. Also, be sure to identify the many things you *get* to do in these new circumstances instead of focusing on what you're restricted from doing. Then, create a new routine around these encouraging activities.

Because ambiguity can also be an incubator for anxiety, establishing a regimen is important. Unstructured time can easily lead to worry, so set a fixed time for exercise. Now is an invaluable opportunity to develop this healthy habit. Also determine clear hours for work, for interaction with family, for regular meals, and certainly for sleep. Plan time for play—and for some interruptions—if you have children at home. The structure you create in your life becomes your skeleton. It can keep you and those you're staying at home with from becoming wobbly in the face of uncertainty. It's the scaffolding that keeps a workday from feeling like a weekend, and vice versa.

Normalize when you're experiencing anxiety on a physical level too. In other words, understand that the situation warrants the biological responses you may be experiencing as well as the emotional ones. In the context of these challenging life events, it's natural for your pupils to dilate, your muscles to tense, or your breathing to accelerate. When this happens, decatastrophize the symptoms by shifting your attention to other things. Imagine some of the fun things you *get* to do while you're home—some of the enjoyments that can be incorporated into your new routine. Allow your mind to roam to all the times you longed to take a bath, enjoy music, read a book, try a new recipe, master a hobby, meditate, learn a new language, or start a new business. Yes, many entrepreneurs made their fortunes by observing what a society in transition needed and moving quickly to provide that service. The Great Recession of 2008, for instance, gave us Airbnb, Karma Credit, and Uber, among other innovative companies, and helped create the gig economy as we know it today. More recently, Josh Boram and Christian Miller, the cofounders of Very Viral Games, created a card game called Covid Survivor that quickly became a #1 bestseller on Amazon. Its tagline states its purpose brilliantly: "Spread fun, not fear." And part of the proceeds from sales is donated to various pandemic-related causes.

With the time you're saving by no longer commuting, you can do such empowering things as these, and more. What long-awaited pursuit will you choose today? Form a mental picture of yourself being resilient. Memorize the details. Is your visualization black-and-white or in color? Your vision should be vivid! How does your body look? How does your posture feel? What does your expression say about what you're experiencing? Imagine putting this image in an album and retrieving it whenever the need, desire, or impulse arises. These visualizations, when transformed into proactive steps, can go a long way toward soothing your anxiety and increasing your mental wellness.

Because anxiety suppresses our immune system, keeping it in check will help maintain our total wellness. Again, understanding helps us to combat anxiety more effectively. For instance, did you know that anxiety, unlike most other mental-health disorders identified in the *DSM-5*, is a late bloomer? While the average age for generalized anxiety disorder to strike is thirty, it can occur for the first time in one's forties, fifties, or sixties too. These are the years when most of us are active in the working world—years when we're typically expected to be responsible, contributing, self-sufficient adults. If you fall into this age category and are experiencing anxiety—even for the first time in your life—know that you're not alone. Others in your cohort are feeling a heightened sense of it, too, particularly if they're staying safe at home and setting a strong example for younger and/or significantly older family members. Some are uncertain if their jobs will be there for them when businesses reopen; others are worried that their businesses, especially in the hospitality and travel industries, will be forced into receivership. Reach out to those in your age bracket on Facebook and other forms of social media to exchange ideas for coping, for encouragement, for an occasional laugh, or even just for a collective sigh.

Know, too, that anxiety and depression often appear together—a neurotic marriage, no doubt! If you find yourself ruminating or getting stuck in an obsessive rut—if you just can't let go of repetitive and annoying thoughts—you're very likely experiencing depression. There's often a component of self-blame to depression; for example, you might wonder whether something you did caused others around you to be upset instead of recognizing that it's likely the circumstances that are getting on everyone's last nerves.

In that case, you may want to try an approach I sometimes take with my clients. Whenever they say such things as, "I know I'm being irrational, but I just can't seem to stop," we both understand that they're stuck in *their* interpretation of events, and that there may be a larger picture to consider. I then ask them to generate another possible interpretation, and, later, a few more possible interpretations. This not only helps them regulate their emotions but also opens them up to comprehending what others around them may be experiencing.

If your mood is still getting in the way of your life in this time of confinement—or at any other time—then you may need more direct professional help. Be aware that even while we're sheltering in place, there are hotlines you can call. In Canada, dial 1-833-456-4566 for Crisis Services Canada, or visit www .crisisservicescanada.ca. Every province has a psychological association that offers assistance for dealing with COVID-19. In the United States, dial 1-800-273-8255 for Mental Health America, Inc., or visit www.mhanational.org. When businesses and schools reopen, some people may be in need of mental health services due to post-traumatic stress disorder (PTSD), acute stress disorder, phobic responses, anxiety, or depression, to cite a few issues. It's important that they reach out for help as well.

*   *   *

There are some potentially negative effects that isolation can have on dysfunctional couples that I feel compelled to discuss here too. Such couples can experience increased distress when they're forced to be in close proximity for long periods of time. Feelings of being trapped can escalate and increase preexisting tensions. Children are also at risk when they're forced to stay at home during the lockdown if their parents are abusive toward them or each other. Physically attending school, going to the playground, or visiting friends were not options for many months. Online interactions between the very young are not necessarily effective experiences. Their ability to tolerate anxiety varies. Isolation can have negative effects on the whole family, and in some cases PTSD may result. There are hotlines one can call in these circumstances as well: in Canada and the United States, call the National Domestic Violence Hotline at 1-800-799-SAFE (7233), or visit www.thehotline.org; in the United Kingdom, call the National Domestic Abuse Helpline at 0808 2000 247, or visit www.nationaldahelpline.org.uk.

One last anxiety-related condition to mention, since it's particularly relevant right now, is phobia. Phobias can be specific and can lead to avoidance. For example, one can have a fear of heights, of flying, of insects, or of animals—and in this time, one can certainly have a fear of germs. Phobias can also be social: one can have a fear of being in a group setting, for instance. Agoraphobia is a fear of being in places from which it's hard to escape or where no immediate help is evident, which includes all public places. Agoraphobia and panic usually occur together. Today, agoraphobia is easier to navigate with physical distancing, self-isolation, online shopping, and access to the

Internet, but the sense of shame that comes with it can make even a short walk outside difficult. After cocooning for so long, those who suffer from agoraphobia may have a hard time coming out of isolation when the stay-at-home mandates are lifted. Helping someone who suffers from this condition to see a therapist would be a kind and helpful gesture when this is over. I don't mention this here to label anyone, but rather to provide a road map to a solution.

While it's true that any preexisting mental problems could be exacerbated by the precautions we all must take against COVID-19, it's a matter of degree and how much they affect your life and your relationships. Bear in mind that just as so many physical ailments are treatable, so are anxiety, depression, panic, and phobias.

Anxiety is certainly prevalent in the United States and Canada. This is partly due to demographics: those with more economic resources report more anxiety, whereas those who are more economically challenged have adjusted to the vicissitudes of their situation and aren't as susceptible to it. We can learn much from them. Recall difficult or untenable experiences you've had in your lifetime. How did you cope? What worked? What didn't work? Then put the memory of those coping strategies in your toolbox so you can use them as needed.

Whatever level your anxiety reaches, know that there are measures you can take to reduce it, ranging from the basic to the creative. The Italians set an example for us when they sang together from their balconies. New Yorkers did, too, when they stood before their windows at the same hour each day, applauding in gratitude for those who risked their safety for us. Surely we can find equivalent unity at every phase of dealing with, treating, and recovering from this event and others if we try. Given the wonders of technology, we can host family and friend gatherings and even enjoy game nights via Zoom. We can share memes and gifs and simple words of encouragement through social media. We can seek the advice of experts through verified websites. We are social *and* adaptive beings at our core, and that won't change. Even in the absence of comforting hugs and warm handshakes, we will continue to find ways to express our togetherness. We may grow to enjoy time spent alone with ourselves as well. Many may learn how to venture inward and perhaps set some long-term goals for themselves and for their communities.

Next Steps

While you're turning your attentions inward, you may ask yourself "What are some of the practices I've developed during this time that I wish to continue?" or "What are some of my new priorities?" After contemplating these questions, you may also want to tackle a few larger issues, including:

How can COVID-19 facilitate our own personal evolution *and* help us establish a new global, interdependent identity? With a bit of courage in the face of a fluid reality, we can create profound change. We can develop in our own unique ways. We can appreciate that each of us is a one-off. And despite the fact that we look different and express our emotions in our own ways, we can also acknowledge that beneath our skin, we all want the same reality: health, connection, and transformation. We can choose to look at how efficient we've already become at using the Internet, teleconferencing, decreasing our consumption, reducing our carbon footprint, and adapting to health care based on triaging, telemedicine, and teletherapy. We can look forward with hope and promise that there are still many other ways to spur healthy transformation of our dystopian reality both as individuals and as a society.

How can we be infected with happiness during COVID-19 or whenever strife may occur in the future? And is there some way we can we become immunized against despair when the rug has been pulled from under our feet?

A few years ago, my husband, Robbie, and I were attending a conference in Cape Town, South Africa. One morning we decided to climb Table Mountain, since the funicular was out of service. On our way down we got hopelessly lost. Without a compass or GPS it became really difficult. Night fell; we were enveloped in darkness. As we walked through several sketchy districts in Cape Town, I felt scared, sore, tired, frustrated, and cold. I was inappropriately dressed in just a pair of running shorts and a T-shirt. All sense of order and direction disappeared for a while, but luckily we relied on our *internal* GPS, got our bearings, and ultimately found our way back to our hotel. Have you ever been lost without a compass or GPS? That's how it has felt for many since the pandemic reached our shores. Life as we know it seems to have disappeared. Our daily routines have been upended, creating a perfect storm for a crisis.

So how do we become infected with happiness in a situation of such sustained ambiguity? I think your internal GPS already knows the answer to this question, especially as you consider all the information you've gathered from this book. We talked earlier, for example, about developing positive addictions; becoming addicted to happiness is certainly one way to navigate these unprecedented times. Once you make some choices, it's just like punching in your coordinates. Your psychological immune system will help you find the way to be happy with those choices.[3] But before we take a look at your many options, let's look at the five countries ranked as the happiest in the world in 2019 for clues about the type of environment where happiness flourishes best. In order, they are:

1. Finland
2. Denmark
3. Switzerland
4. Iceland
5. Norway

Do you know what two important similarities all of these countries share? The answer is trust in public institutions and social connection.[4]

Now, let's take a closer look at some of the characteristics of happy people. You'll recall from chapter nine of this book that genetics accounts for only 50 percent of happiness, and that the main difference between happy people and miserable people is the habits they develop. Happy people engage in more happiness-boosting habits, while miserable people engage in more misery-inducing habits. So here's the good news: you can choose happiness-inducing habits *anytime* and *anywhere*.

These choices can include meditation or mindfulness, as we discussed. (Dr. Dan Siegel, author and founding codirector of the Mindful Awareness Research Center at UCLA, has some excellent exercises in his book *The Developing Mind*.)[5]

Another of my favorite happiness-inducing choices is the practice of engaging in awe. Dacher Keltner, host of the podcast *The Science of Happiness*, recommends looking for experiences that cause goosebumps. He proves experiences that arouse awe can help us reconceptualize our sense of self, our role in society, and our place in the universe.[6] The usefulness of awe in transforming and providing meaning to our challenging experience of COVID-19 seems evident in these words, expressed by Albert Einstein long before the pandemic: "The most beautiful thing we can experience is the mysterious. It is the source of all true art and science. He to whom the emotion is a stranger, who can no longer pause to wonder and stand wrapped in awe, is as good as dead; his eyes are closed."[7] Awe can occur when we look at the simple marvels all around us. It happens when we take a walk after being indoors for long stretches and appreciate nature for a moment that transcends time. Awe can also occur when we see the courage of frontline workers and COVID-19 survivors. Physicians talk about experiencing awe when their cancer patients exhibit grace in the face of death, or, more happily, when their patients recover. Awe overcomes us in response to different stimuli: threat, beauty, ability, virtue, or supernatural phenomena. The experience can be alternately awesome and awful, as we've seen during the COVID-19 crisis. On the one hand, we can experience confusion, fear, and dread; on the other, we can feel appreciation, wonder, and love. Awe forces us to immerse ourselves in the present, which is an effective way to curb anxiety. Keltner's research points to connections between the experience of awe and enhanced creative and critical thinking faculties, improved health, and an increase in prosocial behaviors such as kindness, self-sacrifice, cooperation, and resource sharing.[8] Awe can facilitate the emergence of our global identity during this pandemic.

Expressing gratitude is yet another choice I love. Identifying what makes us grateful and why elevates our mood. This can easily be done at the start or close of each day.

Spending time, money, and energy on others has the positive effect of making us happy too.[9] There are so many pandemic-related causes that could use your contributions. I have also felt greatly rewarded when I've supported people who are finding creative and alternative ways to earn income in this time of increased unemployment. I recently purchased a ticket (for a very nominal fee) to enjoy a live-streamed concert performed by a gifted violinist who has traveled the world playing with various philharmonics but is now relegated to playing solo at home. It was a lovely concert. At moments I felt as if he were playing just for me, though many others were listening too.

Happy people have a great sense of humor as well.[10] Find something to laugh about. The smiles will follow!

Enjoying a nutritious meal also fills a happiness quotient. During this time, many have experienced a fear of food scarcity. By focusing on what you've just eaten, you can take comfort that the next meal will be forthcoming, since you already have the ingredients for another batch or because you've proven you're an ingenious survivor who can creatively pull a meal together from whatever you have in the cupboard. You can share some of your food with others in need, or you can share your creative culinary tips with the rest of us!

You can also take your temperature from time to time. I'm not talking about your bodily temperature, though that is something physicians advise you do when you're feeling any symptoms of COVID-19. Rather, I'm talking about asking yourself the following questions: Is what I'm doing helpful, or is it putting me in danger? Is it healthy or unhealthy? Will it adversely affect anyone else? Do I really need that glass of wine? This practice, when approached with complete honesty, helps you exert more control over your life.

Remember that it's in our DNA to be happy; we're not programmed to be depressed or to worry excessively. When difficulties arise, however, happy people accept that they can't be happy all the time. They understand that suffering is a part of life, and their bouts of depression and anxiety are shorter-lived as a result. Somehow our culture has taught us that we're entitled to have a happy life, that vulnerability is a sign of weakness, that our every need must be met, that we should have guarantees. Happy people understand that this is a false narrative, so when trauma occurs, they don't feel discriminated against. They get it. They see the trauma in the larger context, and that enables them to bounce out of an anxious state quicker than most other people. Try disputing your worries and focus deliberately on what you can change. When you focus only on negative experiences and negative emotions, they stick to you like crazy glue. Conversely, positive emotions and positive experiences wash over you like water off a duck's back. When negative emotions stay with you in the way I've just described, remember that they're a pull toward *negativity bias*. This way of thinking and responding is a holdover from the days when we were hunters and gatherers. It was a survival mechanism intended to help us anticipate and plan for danger. Since we're no longer hunters and gatherers, we no longer need to rely on this strategy so heavily. You're free to relax this instinct when it gets in the way of moving forward—so make a plan for today, follow your routine, and be gentle with yourself. Remember that when you apply water, positive experiences are free to flow; and when you apply glue, you remain stuck in a negative space. So, we need to challenge our negativity bias. As mentioned earlier, we know from neuroplasticity that cells that fire together wire together. The mind can change the brain with lasting positive emotions. Our minds are malleable. Our neural pathways get stronger the more they're used. You can reconfigure your brain to accept happiness in your life by installing positive thinking in your core brain chemistry.[11]

Another uplifting habit is to recount what has gone well for you and why. While this is similar to the practice of gratitude, it differs in that it focuses on how you helped to determine your own good fortune. Martin Seligman found that this particular intervention reduces anxiety and depression because you become aware of how much control you actually have.[12] So go on a treasure hunt for positive memories; it will help you to self-regulate worry and anxiety.

As you can see, our thoughts affect our moods. I'm reminded of an incident that occurred when I was a teenager and was babysitting my younger sister, Anne, who was just three years old at the time. My parents had gone out to a social event. I was engrossed in an Agatha Christie novel when I heard an earsplitting scream. Anne had decided to try out her new red tricycle, which she had christened Melamb. She'd taken her stuffed panda along for the ride and crashed. Once I realized that she hadn't broken any bones, I attempted to get her to stop crying. I told her that she had suddenly become an angel and explained how angels don't experience pain. She began gently spreading her arms the way an angel would spread her wings. Within seconds, Anne was so happy, especially because her bruised wing was moving in sync with her good one. The tears magically stopped, and a glint of joy crept into her eyes. I learned about the power of thought and how it can influence our feelings and behavior at a very young age, and I suspect Anne did as well.

I suggest that you keep a journal of your thoughts and feelings every day, not just for your benefit but for posterity, so others can learn from your experiences and your fortitude. I remember reading *The Diary of a Young Girl* by Anne Frank as a teenager and being so impressed by her resilience and her courage. Storytelling, in which you share your adventures with others and they share theirs with you, is more than a communal conversation; it's also a great stress reducer. Don't forget to complain! Complaining to a like-minded individual, as long as you come up with solutions together, can increase the bond between you—and it's so cathartic!

Also, remember to breathe. Deep breaths slow us down on a physiological level as well as on a mental level.

I enjoy savoring, too, which involves being present in the moment and appreciating whatever it is you're doing. Note the smells, tastes, and feelings you're experiencing, even when you're doing everyday things. This will prevent you from taking even small blessings for granted.

By the way, happy people also tend to experience *flow*—a state in which they're fully immersed in the process of whatever they're doing. You might know it better as being *in the zone*. Do you experience this too? Are you ever so fully immersed in a moment or an activity that time just seems to pass you by? Some experience this when engaged in a sport or while painting or writing. It's a wonderful habit to develop.[13]

Exercise has been proven to reduce stress, so take a walk outside whenever you can. Happy people do this all the time. It doesn't matter if it's only for ten minutes; the secret is to be consistent. Do this daily, and you will surely set yourself up for happiness.

As I mentioned in chapter five, sleep hygiene is important too. At the start of the novel coronavirus pandemic, I had trouble falling asleep, so I changed my nightly ritual. I no longer checked the news after 6:00 p.m.; I put my cell phone on silent after 8:00 p.m.; I took a bath with soothing music playing in the background; and then I selected relaxing audiobooks to listen to as I drifted off to sleep. Try to develop your own self-soothing ritual—one that's brimming with all the benefits of self-care. These practices enhance our self-sufficiency and self-reliance. Many people have reportedly found cooking a delicious meal during lockdown to be relaxing. When their focus is trained on the details of an elaborate recipe, there's no bandwidth left for free-form anxiety and worry. Remember that *thriving* and *productive* aren't necessarily synonymous during these challenging times.

In many ways, this century is typified by the word *productivity*. We've been in such a hurry to get to the finish line that the phrase *slow down* is anathema to us. This behavior has given rise to the term "hurry-up sickness." Slowing down long enough to administer some self-love is vital during these times as we wrestle with anxiety, frustration, irritability, and fear. Can we accept that we're flawed and still regard ourselves with deep respect? Terry Real seems to think so. He calls this self-love and self-esteem, and posits that when we're able to do this, we can transfer the same compassion and love to others, especially when emotions are raw and we're feeling fragile.[14] We're relational beings, after all.

Now that we've reviewed some of the many positive addictions we can adopt in challenging times, it's important to acknowledge the elephant in the room: as with any addiction, we can sometimes fall off the wagon. There are a number of factors in addition to the existence of a deadly virus that can threaten our resolve to stay positive. Certainly the increase in incidents of domestic violence partly due to our confinement is sobering. The rise in deaths of despair from alcoholism and drug abuse also weigh heavily on us, as does the rise in suicides due to unemployment and economic insecurity. In the face of such loss, it may be difficult at times to believe that we can change the tide, but we can. COVID-19 has paradoxically been a catalyst for much good. For instance, it has already spurred greater self-knowledge. It has motivated us to see our interconnectedness and to deal with vital issues that have been simmering beneath the surface—issues that we've failed to deal with for too long. It has also led to greater cooperation. George Floyd's death by police brutality on May 25, 2020, and the ensuing peaceful protests in support of the Black Lives Matter movement have forced us to reexamine the parts we play in systemic racism and economic disparity on a global level. Lockdown has helped reduce our carbon footprint and has also led to more efficient ways of treating patients. We're witnessing acts of courage all over the world and experiencing a collective spirit of generosity. The concerted efforts of scientists to develop a vaccine and to eradicate the virus and the exchange of useful data and protocols in the worldwide medical community are remarkable. These are possible signs of what Viktor Frankl called "tragic optimism," our ability to find meaning in spite of a difficult, untenable situation.[15] In Pamplona, Spain, bullfights have been halted; a change animal activists have been urging for decades!

So, there it is: hints of happiness in chaos. In the Chinese language, the word for chaos means danger *and* opportunity. It's up to us to determine how we'll use the present chaos for growth and the development of resilience, but I'm certain positive addictions will have a role to play.

The Long View

Since the pandemic began, I've often been asked "What's the new normal?" Perhaps, like victims of trauma—which we are— we need to respond to this novel threat by creating a novel way of being. First, we must recognize that we're in a marathon, not a sprint. The old ways are gone. We're already feeling collective and anticipatory grief. Centuries-old traditions, such as in-person funerals, weddings, and graduations, have given way to virtual ones. There's been a loss of normalcy, social connection, and some freedom. And if that's not enough, many of us are walking pathogens! This, however, is where collective resilience comes in. Telling our stories is an effective form of healing. (Get out your journals, people!) A while back, Jack Saul launched a theater project in New York that told the stories of Chilean survivors of torture during the Pinochet regime. The production generated meaningful conversation about what had largely been an unspeakable subject. In fact, it was the very first time that many were able to talk about the trauma. Support from others can help us to become collectively resilient. Now, that's a paradigm shift! When we think of resilience it's usually in individual terms, but recording and sharing our stories actually helps mend many of us at once, and promises to illuminate future generations as well.[16]

We can't return to the lives we once had for a variety of reasons; there have been too many changes to our ways of being. For example, we must rethink how we attend religious services; dine and drink at will in our favorite restaurants and bars; enjoy the services of a hair stylist or barber; partake in concerts, theater, and travel; and, for young people especially, how we build the social skills, independence, and self-confidence typically developed through on-campus interaction with student peers. Shifts in our priorities will occur, if they haven't already. But whatever the challenges, we can always consider a happy, energizing alternative—one that enables us to re-create our lives when our previous ones are no longer possible. What options will you choose while intentionally refashioning the life still ahead of you? Which rituals will you keep? Which will you discard? Which will you reimagine?

This pandemic has us asking another critical question:

Can we face our mortality in a way that actually leaves us more empowered?
Here's the thing: we've spent a considerable number of years focused on the externals. We've obsessed about securing a good job, amassing material wealth, attaining love, and perfecting our bodies, but as the research proves, such things

don't produce the happy result we desire.[17] So, how about sitting down now and writing a brand-new will? Not one that details the stuff you plan to bequeath to others but one that clarifies the legacy you wish to leave behind. I've been doing this very thing since the COVID-19 pandemic began, and I've found it to be extremely liberating. The way I live determines the footprint I leave behind. What remains after I die has everything to do with how I live today. This thinking leads to the crystallization of meaning and purpose, which are at the core of happiness—and, remarkably, at the core of grief as well![18] Sonja Lubormirsky's research[19] points to the happiness advantage for us all. It tells us that our brain works best when we approach any pursuit with positivity. We cannot expect to rise from this present situation with a negative, neutral, or stressed mindset.

Another question I've frequently fielded during this pandemic involves the subject of love. People want to know how to achieve happiness in their relationships during lockdown. Certainly work helps us attune to the rhythm of the world and gives us a temporal sense of life. In the past, we could talk about our commute and the events that occurred throughout the day when we were apart from our loved ones. But being forced to work from home during the pandemic has left many of us with a sense of lost boundaries. Previously, we relied on our village, including extended family, friends, peers, and colleagues, for additional emotional support. Nowadays, we expect the institution of marriage to meet all our needs, and that means everything from erotic needs to needs for security, protection, excitement, acceptance, and companionship. That's a tall order for one person to fill! It's easy to slide down the slippery slope of irritability, anger, criticism, and impatience under such circumstances. Because daily interruptions become the norm, it's important to develop boundaries with your partner. We talked before of setting physical boundaries, such as establishing places within your space for work and socializing, entertainment and play, solitude and sleep, and so forth. To help establish healthy emotional boundaries, let's look now at the ABCs of love.

The *A* in this acronym involves identifying and naming your emotions. In psychology, this is what we call your *affective state*. What are you feeling? Why are you feeling this way?

The *B* stands for behaviors. What are some behaviors of your spouse's or partner's that serve as catalysts for the feelings you're experiencing? Imagine entering a messy kitchen; do you just clean up the mess your partner has made and then have sex with this person later on? What if there's a mess in the kitchen *every day*? Do you use this as ammunition to win some other argument you two may be having? What if you could create a list of your partner's behaviors that leave you feeling upset? What if, after compiling this list, you could approach your partner in a nonthreatening manner and suggest that you talk about one problem each of you is having with the other? The rule for this exchange would be that each of you gets to speak for five minutes with no interruptions. What if, after this exchange, you could devise a mutually acceptable solution? Or perhaps, in your situation, it might be more useful to approach your partner by talking about tasks instead of feelings. For instance, if you're the one who cleans up the kitchen after it's been messed up, you might say any of the following: "I would feel that I really have a partner if

/ I would feel loved if / I would feel appreciated if / I would experience a significant reduction in my anxiety and worry if you would tidy the kitchen after you use it. Can you do that? I realize that this is *my* issue, but when it interferes with my ability to trust you, it becomes *our* issue. Can we sort out a solution that works for you *and* for me?"

Along similar lines, I recall telling my husband one day, "I think I'm in the fast lane to becoming a germaphobe. Now, if you cleaned the counter in the kitchen, I'd feel less anxious and less hyper about sanitizing everything, because I would know and feel reassured that you've done your part to keep me and our family safe." When I broached the topic with my husband in this way, it was like a hot knife through butter. He instantly got it!

So, to recap, in the ABCs of love during lockdown we've identified the emotions we're feeling, and then we've identified the behaviors that cause us discomfort. Lastly, the *C* in this acronym stands for cognitions, thoughts, or expectations: What thoughts bubble up to the surface when you see the behavior that's driving you crazy? Are you perhaps misinterpreting the facts based on your expectations? If this thought occurred to someone else, how would you view the situation? Challenge your expectations. Are you being fair? Are you imposing your values on the other? Look for the tyranny of the "should." Given the situation we're in, it might be more useful to take a deep breath, lower our expectations, and negotiate. Often the behavior will trigger our expectations, and therein lies the mismatch, the misinformation, the jumping to conclusions, the assumption that your partner can read your mind and know exactly what to do. Recognize that your partner might be experiencing anxiety and fears about job loss or about not being an adequate provider, whether that's true or not. How does that translate into behaviors?

Regarding the erotic, many people have asked, "What about imagination? What about sex? What about magic? How do we get rid of boredom and experience novelty again?" Some mystery might be restored by having date nights when the kids are in bed. Change out of your sweatpants, dress up, and make an event out of it, even though you're at home. If you have a competitive mate, you might want to start a game and see who wins at the end of the week. Challenge each other to see who planned the most exciting evening or who baked the best dessert. Be sure to offer prizes for the funniest or most creative efforts. Another expression of love in these times might involve you saying to your mate, "I want to take a walk right now; you look after the kids, and then it will be my turn to watch them so that you can enjoy some individual time as well. I know we both need a break because they're not in school right now." You could negotiate the same way for exercise time too. Sharing close quarters around the clock also presents a fantastic opportunity for you to discover things about your partner that you didn't know before. Overhearing him or her on the telephone as they discuss work-related projects can reveal so much about them that you wouldn't ordinarily have an opportunity to discover.

Bear in mind that now is not the time to make earth-shattering decisions or statements such as, "We need a separation," "I don't trust you," or, "We need to divorce." If you have a problem that can be solved, then you don't have a problem. John Gottman's rules[20] could be quite useful during lockdown. Here are the four rules that I keep posted on my fridge:

- Thou shalt not criticize.
- Thou shalt not stonewall.
- Thou shalt not be defensive.
- Thou shalt not display contempt.

During COVID-19, it's understandable and expected that emotions will be raw at times. We may feel stretched in all directions while going nowhere really fast, especially if our productivity has slowed down. In this day and age, many people will go through more than one relationship in a lifetime. I've been married for twenty-five years, and it's felt like three different relationships with the same person! We need energy, vitality, and aliveness in our relationships. What does your marriage mean to you? Look at your family culture. Is your marriage an economy of service? How do you attempt to fulfill your own needs and the needs of your partner in your marriage? How are you increasing eroticism, adventure, exploration, and excitement during this period of social uncertainty and ambiguity? Now is your opportunity to be creative.

Again, what was normal in relationships before has changed during lockdown, because while we still live in a relational world, all our roles now overlap in the same place. In my situation, that place is typically around the kitchen table. From an enlightened position of self-interest, we can proceed happily through our new reality by devising an arrangement that works for both partners; we can have that task conversation with each other, and include our children too. We can create a house chart of complaints that we post on the fridge so everyone becomes part of the solution. We can learn how to deal with our emotions, behaviors, and expectations through the art of negotiation. We can have the feelings talk with other people in our lives as well, if we think it might yield more rewarding interactions. My go-to question is usually, "What do you think we could do better?" I use humor, stick to the topic, and avoid character assassination. I usually start with the following: "I feel _____ when you do _____." I try to avoid labeling, and I definitely steer clear of bringing up the past. I stay focused on how the behaviors leave me with negative feelings, especially when I see inequality, neglect, or lack of trust. For instance, those whose partners are lax about following medical experts' advice might say, "When you go out and don't wear a mask, that shows me your disregard for the well-being of others, but I know you care for me, so is this something that you might consider changing with me and my many anxieties and insecurities in mind?" Usually an apology will follow, and, at best, an epiphany or a new understanding will occur. You might even hear the words "I never thought of it that way."

So, those are my ABCs of love. What additional and creative ideas do you have? Reflect on your experiences in your journal.

As part of your conscious transformation in these times, also remember to become addicted to kindness. And that, by the way, includes being kind to yourself. In his 1871 book *The Descent of Man*, Charles Darwin argued that sympathy would increase through natural selection, and that communities including the greatest number of highly sympathetic members would produce and rear the greatest number of offspring; thus, human societies with the most sympathetic members would flourish. COVID-19 gives us the opportunity to focus on human goodness instead of self-interest, to concentrate on interdependence, to show compassion above all—especially to ourselves when we're feeling vulnerable—and to evidence "survival of the kindest."[21]

So how about our collectively exercising this survival instinct? It may well lead to a post-traumatic global identity in which we value cooperation over competition and prioritize the well-being of others as a means of ensuring the well-being of the whole. This global identity we're poised to create is one in which we value the health and well-being of everyone. Happiness will follow when we give back!

Like the butterfly pupa in the chrysalis, we can break out of our "old normal," discard the things that didn't serve us well, harness our emotions, and emerge from our silken prison to direct our energies toward the development of our post-traumatic, globally interdependent identity. The young butterfly's wings are still wet and fragile, but as it ascends above the trees, it grows stronger and more confident. The world looks the same from up there, yet it is already very different.

works consulted

Chapter One: Chasing Happiness

Ackerman, Courtney E., MSc. "What Is Happiness and Why Is It Important?" PositivePsychology.com, April 15, 2020, https://positivepsychology.com/what-is-happiness/.

Cohen, Ilene Strauss, PhD. "Is the Pursuit of Happiness a Source of Unhappiness?" *Psychology Today*, May 30, 2017, https://www.psychologytoday.com/us/blog/your-emotional-meter/201705/is-the-pursuit-happiness-source-unhappiness.

Dewey, Caitlin. "A Fascinating Map of the World's Happiest and Least Happy Countries." *Washington Post*, September 10, 2103, https://www.washingtonpost.com/news/worldviews/wp/2013/09/10/a-fascinating-map-of-the-worlds-happiest-and-least-happy-countries/.

Ducharme, Jamie. "Trying to Be Happy Is Making You Miserable. Here's Why." *Time*, August 10, 2018, https://time.com/5356657/trying-to-be-happy/.

Dunn, Elizabeth, and Michael Norton. *Happy Money: The Science of Happier Spending*. New York: Simon & Schuster, 2013.

Grant, Adam. "Want Happiness? Science Says You Should Stop Looking for It." Fulfillment Daily, July 28, 2014, http://www.fulfillmentdaily.com/want-happiness-science-says-stop-looking/.

Gruber, June. "Four Ways Happiness Can Hurt You." *Greater Good Magazine*, May 3, 2012, https://greatergood.berkeley.edu/article/ item/four_ways_happiness_can_hurt_you.

Gruber, June, Aleksandr Kogan, Jordi Quoidbach, and Iris B. Mauss. "Happiness Is Best Kept Stable: Positive Emotion Variability Is Associated with Poorer Psychological Health." *Emotion* 13, no. 1 (2013): 1–6; https://www.apa.org/pubs/journals/features/emo -a0030262.pdf.

Haas, Michaela, PhD. "Why Striving for Happiness Can Make You Unhappy." PsychCentral.com, July 8, 2018, https://psychcentral. com/blog/why-striving-for-happiness-can-make-you-unhappy/.

"A Harvard Study: The Science of Happiness." Ignitia Office, January 3, 2020, https://www.ignitiaoffice.com/the-science-of-happiness -a-harvard-study/.

Jackson, McKenna. "The Endless Pursuit of Happiness." Odyssey, October 3, 2017, https://www.theodysseyonline.com/endless -pursuit-happiness.

Mauss, Iris B., Maya Tamir, Craig L. Anderson, and Nicole S. Savino. "Can Seeking Happiness Make People Unhappy? Paradoxical Effects of Valuing Happiness." *Emotion* 11, no. 4 (August 2011): 807–15; https://www.ncbi.nlm.nih.gov/pubmed/21517168.

McKee, Annie. "Being Happy at Work Matters." *Harvard Business Review*, November 14, 2014, https://hbr.org/2014/11/being -happy-at-work-matters.

"The Pursuit of Happiness." Pathway to Happiness, August 26, 2019, https://pathwaytohappiness.com/blog/the-pursuit-of-happiness/.

Scott, Elizabeth, MS. "Hedonic Adaptation: Why You Are Not Happier." VeryWell Mind, May 4, 2019, https://www .verywellmind.com/hedonic-adaptation-4156926.

Scotti, Dan. "Why Your Constant Search For Happiness Is Actually Making You Unhappy." Elite Daily, November 9, 2015, https:// www.elitedaily.com/life/search-for-happiness/1276087.

Whippman, Ruth. "America Is Obsessed with Happiness—and It's Making Us Miserable." *Vox*, October 4, 2016, https://www.vox .com/first-person/2016/10/4/13093380/happiness-america-ruth -whippman.

Chapter Two: Compare at Your Own Risk

Cherry, Kendra. "Social Comparison Theory in Psychology." VeryWell Mind, May 1, 2020, https://www.verywellmind.com/what-is-the -social-comparison-process-2795872.

"The Danger of Comparing Yourself to Others." *Farnham Street* (blog), https://fs.blog/2019/06/comparing-yourself-others/.

"More Men Undergo Plastic Surgery as the Daddy-Do-Over Trend Rises in Popularity." Press release, American Society of Plastic Surgeons, June 12, 2019, https://www.plasticsurgery.org/news/ press-releases/more-men-undergo-plastic-surgery-as-the-daddy -do-over-trend-rises-in-popularity.

Sreenivasan, Shoba, PhD, and Linda E. Weinberger, PhD. "The Digital Psychological Disconnect." *Psychology Today*, July 10, 2016, https://www.psychologytoday.com/us/blog/emotional- nourishment/201607/the-digital-psychological-disconnect.

Stenvinkel, Maria. "13 Things to Do Instead of Comparing Yourself to Others." Tiny Buddha, https://tinybuddha.com/blog/13-things -instead-comparing-others/.

Summerville, Amy, PhD. "Is Comparison Really the Thief of Joy?" *Psychology Today*, March 21, 2019, https://www.psychologytoday .com/us/blog/multiple-choice/201903/is-comparison-really-the -thief-joy.

Tversky, Amos, and Daniel Kahneman. "Judgment under Uncertainty: Heuristics and Biases." *Science* 185, no. 4157 (September 27, 1974): 1124–31; doi:10.1126/science.185.4157.1124.

Webber, Rebecca. "The Comparison Trap." *Psychology Today*, November 7, 2017, https://www.psychologytoday.com/us/ articles/201711/the-comparison-trap.

"Why Do We Tend to Think That Things That Happened Recently Are More Likely to Happen Again?" Decision Lab, https://thedecisionlab.com/biases/availability-heuristic.

Wiebe, David Andrew. "Comparison Is the Root of All Unhappiness." Medium, August 29, 2018, https://medium.com/@davidawiebe/comparison-is-the-root-of-all-unhappiness-90b9bbafbda1.

Chapter Three: Loneliness

Bialik, Kristen. "Americans Unhappy with Family, Social or Financial Life Are More Likely to Say They Feel Lonely." Pew Research Center, December 3, 2018, https://www.pewresearch.org/fact-tank/2018/12/03/americans-unhappy-with-family-social-or-financial-life-are-more-likely-to-say-they-feel-lonely/.

Brownstein, Joe. "Want to Be Happy? Stop Trying." Live Science, May 19, 2011, https://www.livescience.com/14229-happiness-factors.html.

Brueck, Hilary. "We're Learning More about How Social Isolation Damages Your Brain and Body—Here Are the Biggest Effects." Business Insider, July 3, 2018, https://www.businessinsider.com/why-loneliness-bad-brain-body-what-to-do-2018-5.

DiJulio, Bianca, Liz Hamel, Cailey Munana, and Mollyann Drodie. "Loneliness and Social Isolation in the United States, the United Kingdom, and Japan: An International Survey." Kaiser Family Foundation, August 30, 2018, https://www.kff.org/report-section/loneliness-and-social-isolation-in-the-united-states-the-united-kingdom-and-japan-an-international-survey-section-1/.

Dunkelman, Marc J. *The Vanishing Neighbor: The Transformation of American Community.* New York: W. W. Norton & Company, 2014.

Economic Development Curmudgeon. "The Vanishing Neighbor." *Journal of Applied Research in Economic Development*, nd, http://journal.c2er.org/2015/02/the-vanishing-neighbor/.

Friday, Francesca. "More Americans Are Single Than Ever Before—
and They're Healthier, Too." *Observer*, January 16, 2018, https://
observer.com/2018/01/more-americans-are-single-than-ever
-before-and-theyre-healthier-too/.

Holt-Lunstad, Julianne, PhD. "The Potential Public Health
Relevance of Social Isolation and Loneliness: Prevalence,
Epidemiology, and Risk Factors." *Public Policy and Aging Report*
27, no. 4 (2017): 127–30; https://academic.oup.com/ppar/
article/27/4/127/4782506.

Holt-Lunstad, Julianne, PhD, Timothy B. Smith, Mark Baker, Tyler
Harris, and David Stephenson. "Loneliness and Social Isolation
as Risk Factors for Mortality: A Meta-Analytic Review." BYU
ScholarsArchive, March 23, 2015, https://scholarsarchive.byu.
edu/cgi/viewcontent.cgi?article=3024&context=facpub.

Jones, Jeffrey M. "U.S. Church Membership Down Sharply in Past
Two Decades." Gallup, April 18, 2019, https://news.gallup.com/
poll/248837/church-membership-down-sharply-past-two
-decades.aspx.

Khullar, Dhruv. "How Social Isolation Is Killing Us." *New York Times*,
December 22, 2016, https://www.nytimes.com/2016/12/22/
upshot/how-social-isolation-is-killing-us.html.

Mental Health Information—Statistics—Suicide. National Institute
of Mental Health, April 2019, https://www.nimh.nih.gov/health/
statistics/suicide.shtml.

"New Cigna Study Reveals Loneliness at Epidemic Levels in America."
Cigna.com, May 1, 2018, https://www.cigna.com/newsroom/
news-releases/2018/new-cigna-study-reveals-loneliness-at
-epidemic-levels-in-america.

"1 in 3 Americans Can't Eat a Meal without Being on Their Phone."
Nutrisystem Newsroom, January 23, 2018, https://newsroom.
nutrisystem.com/1-in-3-americans-cant-eat-a-meal-without
-being-on-their-phone/.

Ozcelik, Hakan, and Sigal Barsade. "No Employee an Island: Workplace Loneliness and Job Performance." *Academy of Management Journal* 61, no. 6 (February 2018), https://www.researchgate.net/publication/323007916_No_employee_an_island_Workplace_loneliness_and_job_performance.

Reinking, K., and R. Bell. "Relationships among Loneliness, Communication Competence, and Career Success in a State Bureaucracy: A Field Study of the 'Lonely at the Top' Maxim," *Communication Quarterly* 39, no. 4 (1991): 358–73.

Renner, Ben. "Smartphone Addiction Increases Loneliness, Isolation; No Different from Substance Abuse, Experts Say." StudyFinds, April 19, 2018, https://www.studyfinds.org/smartphone-addiction-loneliness-isolation-substance-abuse/.

Rokach, Ami, ed. *Loneliness Updated: Recent Research on Loneliness and How It Affects Our Lives.* New York: Routledge, 2013.

Roxburgh, Alan. "Book Review: *The Vanishing Neighbor: The Transformation of American Community* by Marc J. Dunkleman." *Journal of Missional Practice,* Winter 2015, https://journalofmissionalpractice.com/book-review-the-vanishing-neighbor-the-transformation-of-american-community-culture-by-marc-j-dunkelman/.

Schulze, Hannah. "Loneliness: An Epidemic?" *Science in the News* (blog), April 16, 2018, http://sitn.hms.harvard.edu/flash/2018/loneliness-an-epidemic/.

Sherwood, Chris, Dr. Dylan Kneale, and Barbara Bloomfield. "The Way We Are Now." Relate, August 2014, https://www.relate.org.uk/sites/default/files/publication-way-we-are-now-aug2014_1.pdf.

Siegel, Larry J., and Chris McCormick. *Criminology in Canada: Theories, Patterns, and Typologies.* 3rd ed. Toronto: Thompson Educational Publishing, 2006.

Snyder, Anne. "Family and *The Vanishing Neighbor.*" Institute for Family Studies, December 22, 2014, https://ifstudies.org/blog/family-and-the-vanishing-neighbor.

Waldinger, Robert, MD, dir. "Harvard Study of Adult Development."
https://www.adultdevelopmentstudy.org/.

Chapter Four: Negative Addictions

Bennett, Carole, MA. "The Road to Addiction: Loneliness and
Depression." *HuffPost*, November 17, 2011, https://www.huffpost.
com/entry/the-road-to-addiction---1_b_232674.

Blakemore, Erin. "Neuroscientist Thinks One Way to Fight Opioid
Addiction Is to Tackle Loneliness." *Washington Post*, December 1,
2018, https://www.washingtonpost.com/national/health-science/
neuroscientist-thinks-one-way-to-fight-opioid-addiction-is
-to-tackle-loneliness/2018/11/30/8f651440-f33d-11e8-80d0
-f7e1948d55f4_story.html.

Boyle, Matthew. "Why Addicts Are Often Lonely People."
PsychCentral.com, June 27, 2018, https://psychcentral.com/blog/
why-addicts-are-often-lonely-people/.

"The Connection between Loneliness & Substance Abuse." Lasting
Recovery, nd, https://lastingrecovery.com/the-connection
-between-loneliness-and-substance-abuse/.

"The Connection between Loneliness and Substance Abuse." Simple
Recovery, July 26, 2018, https://www.simplerecovery.com/the
-connection-between-loneliness-and-substance-abuse/.

Dolan, Michael. "Loneliness and Other Digital Addiction Symptoms
Are Seen in Students." Everyday Health, April 4, 2018, https://
www.everydayhealth.com/addiction/loneliness-other-digital
-addiction-symptoms-are-seen-students/.

"Drugs, Brains, and Behavior: The Science of Addiction." National
Institute on Drug Abuse, July 2020, https://www.drugabuse.
gov/publications/drugs-brains-behavior-science-addiction/drug
-misuse-addiction.

Ferry, Tom, with Laura Morton. *Life! By Design: 6 Steps to an
Extraordinary You*. New York: Ballantine Books, 2010.

"How Loneliness Fuels Addiction." Recovery Centers of America, nd, https://recoverycentersofamerica.com/blogs/how-loneliness-fuels-addiction/.

Jane. "6 Core Human Needs by Anthony Robbins." Habits for Wellbeing, nd, https://www.habitsforwellbeing.com/6-core-human-needs-by-anthony-robbins/.

Marty, Meghan A., and Daniel L. Segal. "*DSM-5*" in *Encyclopedia of Clinical Psychology*, Robin L. Cautin and Scott O. Lilienfeld, eds. Hoboken, NJ: Wiley-Blackwell, 2015; https://www.researchgate.net/publication/283296361_DSM-5_Diagnostic_and_Statistical_Manual_of_Mental_Disorders.

Perel, Esther. "The State of Affairs: Rethinking Infidelity." EstherPerel.com, nd, https://www.estherperel.com/store/the-state-of-affairs.

R., Mary. "The Paradox of Loneliness in Addiction." *Crossroads* (blog), March 5, 2017, https://crossroadsnaples.org/the-paradox-of-loneliness-in-addiction/.

Schreiber, Shari, MA. "Outgrowing Your Addiction." ShariSchreiber.com, nd, https://sharischreiber.com/outgrowing-your-addiction/.

Spröte, Patrick, and Rolan W. Fleming. "Concavities, Negative Parts, and the Perception That Shapes Are Complete." *Journal of Vision* 13, no. 14 (December 4, 2013): 3, https://pubmed.ncbi.nlm.nih.gov/24306852/.

Steingold, Daniel. "College Students 'Constantly' on Phones during Class, Study Finds." StudyFinds.org, October 27, 2017, https://www.studyfinds.org/college-students-smartphones-lectures/.

Study Finds. "1 in 3 Can't Get through Meal Without Looking at Phone, Survey Finds." StudyFinds.org, February 15, 2018, https://www.studyfinds.org/phone-eating-meal-distracted/.

Vance, Erik. "What Screen Addictions and Drug Addictions Have in Common." NOVA, PBS.org, October 23, 2018, https://www.pbs.org/wgbh/nova/article/screen-time-addiction/.

Chapter Five: The Value of Connection

"Alone Time vs. Isolation: How to Find the Balance." HealthiNation, February 13, 2019, https://www.healthination.com/health/alone -time-vs-isolation.

Clay, Rebecca A. "Stumbling on Happiness." *Monitor on Psychology* 41, no. 5 (May 2010): 28; https://www.apa.org/monitor/2010/05/ happiness.

Freedman, Joshua. "The Six Seconds Model." 6Seconds.org, nd, http:// admin.6seconds.org/pdf/The_Six_Seconds_Model.pdf.

Gotter, Ana. "8 Breathing Exercises to Try When You Feel Anxious." Healthline, April 22, 2019, https://www.healthline.com/health/ breathing-exercises-for-anxiety.

Hurst, Katherine. "What Is Self-Care and Why Is Self-Care Important?" TheLawofAttraction.com, nd, https://www .thelawofattraction.com/self-care-tips/.

Kahneman, Daniel, Alan B. Krueger, David A. Schkade, Norbert Schwarz, and Arthur A. Stone. "A Survey Method for Characterizing Daily Life Experience: The Day Reconstruction Method." *Science* 306, no. 5702 (December 3, 2004): 1776–80; https://www.ncbi.nlm.nih.gov/pubmed/15576620.

Lender, Dafna. "Tuning into Attunement." *Psychotherapy Networker*, January/February 2018, https://www.psychotherapynetworker .org/magazine/article/1137/tuning-into-attunement.

Lisitsa, Ellie. "Emotional Attunement." Gottman Institute, January 16, 2014, https://www.gottman.com/blog/self-care-emotional -attunement/.

Popova, Maria. "The Central Paradox of Love: Esther Perel on Reconciling the Closeness Needed for Intimacy with the Psychological Distance That Fuels Desire." Brain Pickings, https:// www.brainpickings.org/2016/10/13/mating-in-captivity-esther -perel/.

Saum, Carrie. "Basic Attunement: How Do I Start Listening to What My Own Self Is Trying to Tell Me?" Ravishly, May 21, 2020, https://ravishly.com/basic-attunement-how-do-i-start-listening-what-my-own-self-trying-tell-me.

"Sleep and Mental Health." Harvard Health Publishing, March 18, 2019, https://www.health.harvard.edu/newsletter_article/sleep-and-mental-health.

Tartakovsky, Margarita, MS. "5 Ways to Strengthen Your Connection to Yourself." PsychCentral.com, July 8, 2018, https://psychcentral.com/blog/5-ways-to-strengthen-your-connection-to-yourself/.

Chapter Six: Connecting with Others

Asamoah, Tracy, MD. "Finding Personal Connection in a Disconnected World." *Psychology Today*, April 2, 2018, https://www.psychologytoday.com/us/blog/lets-reconnect/201804/finding-personal-connection-in-disconnected-world.

Barron, Carrie, MD. "8 Ways to Really Connect with Each Other." *Psychology Today*, September 30, 2015, https://www.psychologytoday.com/us/blog/the-creativity-cure/201509/8-ways-really-connect-each-other.

Chernyak, Paul, LPC. "How to Build Social Connections When You Have Depression." wikiHow, June 26, 2019, https://www.wikihow.com/Build-Social-Connections-when-You-Have-Depression.

Dodgson, Lindsay. "It Takes Roughly 200 Hours to Become Best Friends with Someone, According to Science." *Business Insider*, April 7, 2018, https://www.businessinsider.com/how-long-it-takes-to-be-best-friends-with-someone-2018-4.

Friar, Sarah. "How Neighborhood Connections Are Helping Combat Social Isolation and Loneliness." Thrive Global, July 22, 2019, https://thriveglobal.com/stories/how-neighborhood-connections-are-helping-combat-social-isolation-and-loneliness/.

Hajdari, Anduena. "The Importance of Deep and Meaningful Relationships." Medium, October 11, 2018, https://medium.

com/@ena.hajdari95/the-importance-of-deep-and-meaningful
-relationships-b0c476f0a472.

Hood, Kate. "The Benefits of Active Constructive Responding."
Institute of Positive Education, https://www.ggs.vic.edu.au/Blog
-Posts/the-benefits-of-active-constructive-responding.

Lauriston, Ursula. "5 Ways the Incredibly Well-Connected Build
Social Capital." Ladders, October 29, 2018, https://www
.theladders.com/career-advice/5-ways-the-incredibly-well
-connected-build-social-capital.

McGonigal, Kelly. *The Upside of Stress: Why Stress Is Good for You, and
How to Get Good at It*. Kindle edition. New York: Penguin, 2015.

McGuire-Snieckus, Rebecca, Dr., and Nigel Holt. "Can You Make Real
Friends Online?" Psychologies, January 31, 2018, https://www
.psychologies.co.uk/self/friends-online.html.

Oldenburg, Ray. *The Great Good Place*. Kindle edition. New York:
Da Capo Press, 1989.

Putnam, Robert D. "Social Capital Primer." RobertDPutnam.com, nd,
http://robertdputnam.com/bowling-alone/social-capital-primer/.

Society for Personality and Social Psychology. "Meaningful Relationships
Can Help You Thrive." *ScienceDaily*, August 29, 2014, https://www
.sciencedaily.com/releases/2014/08/140829084247.htm.

"*The Great Good Place* (book)." Wikipedia, nd, https://en.wikipedia
.org/wiki/The_Great_Good_Place_(book).

"*The Human Story*." GoodReads, nd, https://www.goodreads.com/
book/show/1144138.The_Human_Story.

"Threat or Challenge? The Surprising New Science of How We
Think about Stress." Six Seconds, nd, https://www.6seconds
.org/2019/04/16/threat-or-challenge-the-surprising-new-science
-of-how-we-think-about-stress/.

Weiss, Robert, PhD. "The Opposite of Addiction Is Connection."
Psychology Today, September 30, 2015, https://www
.psychologytoday.com/us/blog/love-and-sex-in-the-digital-
age/201509/the-opposite-addiction-is-connection.

Chapter Seven: A Bend in the Road Is Not the End of the Road

Ackerman, Courtney E., MSc. "Cognitive Distortions: When Your Brain Lies to You (+ PDF Worksheets)." Positive Psychology, April 15, 2020, https://positivepsychology.com/cognitive-distortions/.

Beck, Aaron T. *Cognitive Therapy and the Emotional Disorders.* New York: Penguin, 1979; https://books.google.com/books/about/Cognitive_Therapy_and_the_Emotional_Diso.html?id=nSFvAAAAQBAJ.

Burns, David D., MD. Feeling Good (website), https://feelinggood.com/.

Foran, Caroline. "6 Cognitive Distortions That Could Be Fueling Your Anxious Thoughts." Health.com, April 16, 2019, https://www.health.com/condition/anxiety/cognitive-distortions.

GoodTherapy Staff. "20 Cognitive Distortions and How They Affect Your Life." GoodTherapy, April 7, 2015, https://www.goodtherapy.org/blog/20-cognitive-distortions-and-how-they-affect-your-life-0407154.

Grohol, John M., PsyD. "15 Common Cognitive Distortions." PsychCentral.com, June 24, 2019, https://psychcentral.com/lib/15-common-cognitive-distortions/.

"Polarized Thinking: A Cognitive Distortion." Exploring Your Mind, February 16, 2019, https://exploringyourmind.com/polarized-thinking-cognitive-distortion/.

Zeig, Jeffrey K., PhD, and Joan Neehall, PhD. *The Habit of a Happy Life: 30 Days to a Positive Addiction.* Phoenix, AZ: Zeig, Tucker & Theisen, Inc., 2017.

Chapter Eight: Positive Addictions

Berne, Eric. *Transactional Analysis in Psychotherapy.* Castle Books, 1961.

Gartrell, Dan, Dr. "Readiness: Not a State of Knowledge, but a State of Mind." National Association for the Education of Young Children,

2013, https://families.naeyc.org/learning-and-development/child
-development/readiness-not-state-knowledge-state-mind.

Glasser, William, MD. *Positive Addiction*. New York: Harper
Perennial, 1976.

Goetzke, Kathryn. "Is There Such a Thing as Positive Addiction?
Dr. Glasser Thinks So, But Do You?" PsychCentral.com, June
22, 2010, https://blogs.psychcentral.com/adhd/2010/06/
is-there-such-a-thing-as-positive-addiction-dr-glasser-thinks
-so-but-do-you/.

O'Connor, Peg, PhD. "Are There Positive Addictions?" *Psychology
Today*, November 19, 2014, https://www.psychologytoday.com/
us/blog/philosophy-stirred-not-shaken/201411/are-there-positive
-addictions.

Sharma, Roma. "Understanding Our Ego States." Medium, November
10, 2017, https://medium.com/romasharma/understanding-our
-ego-states-77893182c269.

Tester, Leonard. "Can Addiction Be Positive?" *Brain World*, November
12, 2017, https://brainworldmagazine.com/can-addiction-positive/.

Toren, Adam. "5 Ways You Can Develop a Positive Addiction to
Success." Entrepreneur.com, August 4, 2015, https://www
.entrepreneur.com/article/248809.

"Transactional Analysis." Wikipedia, nd, https://en.wikipedia.org/
wiki/Transactional_analysis.

Zeig, Jeffrey K., PhD, and Joan Neehall, PhD. *The Habit of a Happy
Life: 30 Days to a Positive Addiction*. Phoenix, AZ: Zeig, Tucker &
Theisen, Inc., 2017.

Chapter Nine: Motivation for a Happier Life

"Affective Forecasting." Wikipedia, nd, https://en.wikipedia.org/wiki/
Affective_forecasting.

Becker, Joshua. "How to Be Happy: 8 Ways to Be Happier Today."
BecomingMinimalist.com, December 21, 2019, https://www
.becomingminimalist.com/how-to-be-happy/.

———. "9 Places Unhappy People Look for Happiness."
BecomingMinimalist.com, nd, https://www.becomingminimalist
.com/be-happy/.

Dixit, Jay. "The Art of Now: Six Steps to Living in the Moment."
Psychology Today, June 9, 2016, https://www.psychologytoday
.com/us/articles/200811/the-art-now-six-steps-living-in-the
-moment.

Gilbert, D. T., and Timothy D. Wilson. "Miswanting: Some Problems
in the Forecasting of Future Affective States" in *Thinking and
Feeling: The Role of Affect in Social Cognition*, edited by Joseph P.
Forgas, 178–97. Cambridge: Cambridge University Press, 2000;
https://dash.harvard.edu/handle/1/14549983.

"How Does Misfortune Affect Long-Term Happiness?" *TED
Radio Hour*, NPR, February 14, 2014, https://www.npr.org/
transcripts/271144389.

Ivey, A. E., N. B. Gluckstern, and M. B. Ivey. *Basic Influencing Skills*.
3rd ed. Amherst, MA: Microtraining Associates, 1997.

Khoddam, Rubin, PhD. "What's Your Definition of Happiness?"
Psychology Today, June 16, 2015, https://www.psychologytoday.
com/us/blog/the-addiction-connection/201506/whats-your
-definition-happiness.

Lyubomirsky, Sonja. *The How of Happiness: A New Approach to
Getting the Life You Want*. New York: Penguin, 2008; http://
thehowofhappiness.com/.

Marshall, Lisa. "The Flip Side of Happiness." *Coloradan*, February
11, 2019, https://www.colorado.edu/coloradan/2018/12/01/
psychology-happiness-june-gruber.

Michalec, Elizabeth M., et al. "A Cocaine Negative Consequences
Checklist: Development and Validation." *Journal of Substance
Abuse* 8, no. 2 (1996): 181–93; https://www.sciencedirect.com/
science/article/abs/pii/S0899328996902382.

Miller, William R., PhD. *Enhancing Motivation for Change in
Substance Abuse Treatment*. Rockville, MD: Center for Substance

Abuse Treatment, US Department of Health and Human Services, 1999.

Robbins, Mel. *The 5 Second Rule: Transform Your Life, Work, and Confidence with Everyday Courage.* Kindle edition. Nashville, TN: Savio Republic, 2017.

Seligman, Martin E. P., PhD. *Authentic Happiness: Using the New Positive Psychology to Realize Your Potential for Lasting Fulfillment.* Kindle edition. New York: Free Press, 2002.

Sobell, L. C., M. B. Sobell, T. Toneatto, and G. I. Leo. "What Triggers the Resolution of Alcohol Problems without Treatment?" *Alcoholism, Clinical and Experimental Research* 17, no. 2 (April 1993): 217–24.

Substance Abuse and Mental Health Services Administration Center for Substance Abuse Treatment. *Enhancing Motivation for Change in Substance Abuse Treatment.* Rockville, MD: SAMHSA, 1999; https://www.ncbi.nlm.nih.gov/books/NBK64972/.

Tamir, Maya. "Secret to Happiness May Include More Unpleasant Emotions." American Psychological Association, August 14, 2017, https://www.apa.org/news/press/releases/2017/08/secret-happiness.

Tucker, J. A., R. E. Vuchinich, and J. A. Gladsjo. "Environmental Events Surrounding Natural Recovery from Alcohol-Related Problems." *Journal of Studies on Alcohol* 55, no. 4 (July 1994): 401–11.

Tucker-Ladd, Clayton E., Dr. "Chapter 4: Behavior, Motivation and Self-Control." In *Psychological Self-Help*, by Dr. Clayton E. Tucker-Ladd. Self-pub, 1996; http://www.psychologicalselfhelp.org/Chapter4/chap4_47.html.

Varney, S. M., D. J. Rohsenow, A. N. Dey, M. G. Myers, W. R. Zwick, and P. M. Monti. "Factors Associated with Help Seeking and Perceived Dependence among Cocaine Users." *American Journal of Drug and Alcohol Abuse* 21, no. 1 (February 1995): 81–91.

Chapter Ten: Becoming an Ingenious Survivor during Dystopian Times

Berinato, Scott. "That Discomfort You're Feeling Is Grief." *Harvard Business Review*, March 23, 2020, https://hbr.org/2020/03/that-discomfort-youre-feeling-is-grief.

Csikszentmihalyi, Mihaly. *Flow: The Psychology of Optimal Experience*. New York: Harper & Row, 1990.

Douyon, Philippe, MD. *Neuroplasticity: Your Brain's Superpower*. Salt Lake City, UT: Izzard Ink, 2019.

Epel, Elissa. "Coping with Coronavirus: An Upside of Anxiety, the Curse of Panic." *San Francisco Chronicle*, March 18, 2020, https://www.sfchronicle.com/openforum/article/How-to-turn-the-coronavirus-anxiety-into-15136037.php.

Frankl, Viktor E. *Man's Search for Meaning*. Vienna: Verlag für Jugend und Volk, 1946.

Gilbert, Daniel. *Stumbling on Happiness*. New York: Alfred A. Knopf, 2006.

Gottman, John, PhD. *Why Marriages Succeed or Fail: And How You Can Make Yours Last*. New York: Simon & Schuster, 1994.

High, Emily. "Navigating Happiness amidst COVID-19; Key Outcomes from World Happiness Report Webinar." Sustainable Development Solutions Network, March 23, 2020, https://www.unsdsn.org/navigating-happiness-amidst-covid-19-key-outcomes-from-world-happiness-report-webinar.

Keltner, Dacher. "Why Do We Feel Awe?" Mindful, May 11, 2016, https://www.mindful.org/why-do-we-feel-awe/.

Kessler, David. *Finding Meaning: The Sixth Stage of Grief*. New York: Scribner, 2019.

Kukk, Christopher. "Survival of the Fittest Has Evolved; Try Survival of the Kindest." Better by *Today*, March 8, 2017, https://www.nbcnews.com/better/relationships/survival-fittest-has-evolved-try-survival-kindest-n730196.

Lyubomirsky, Sonja. *The How of Happiness: A Scientific Approach to Getting the Life You Want*. New York: Penguin, 2007.

Real, Terrence. *The New Rules of Marriage: What You Need to Know to Make Love Work*. New York: Ballantine Books, 2007.

Saul, Jack. *Collective Trauma, Collective Healing: Resilience in the Aftermath of Disaster*. New York: Routledge, 2014.

Seligman, Martin E. P., PhD. *Authentic Happiness: Using the New Positive Psychology to Realize Your Potential for Lasting Fulfillment*. Kindle edition. New York: Free Press, 2002.

Siegel, Daniel J. *The Developing Mind: How Relationships and the Brain Interact to Shape Who We Are*. New York: Guilford Press, 1999.

Stone, Emma, PhD. "The Emerging Science of Awe and Its Benefits." *Psychology Today*, April 27, 2017, https://www.psychologytoday.com/us/blog/understanding-awe/201704/the-emerging-science-awe-and-its-benefits.

notes

Chapter One: Chasing Happiness

1 June Gruber, "Four Ways Happiness Can Hurt You," *Greater Good Magazine*, May 3, 2012, https://greatergood.berkeley.edu/article/item/four_ways_happiness_can_hurt_you.

2 Elizabeth Dunn and Michael Norton, *Happy Money: The Science of Happier Spending* (New York: Simon & Schuster, 2013).

Chapter Two: Compare at Your Own Risk

1 "More Men Undergo Plastic Surgery as the Daddy-Do-Over Trend Rises in Popularity," press release, American Society of Plastic Surgeons, June 12, 2019, https://www.plasticsurgery.org/news/press-releases/more-men-undergo-plastic-surgery-as-the-daddy-do-over-trend-rises-in-popularity.

2 "Why Do We Tend to Think That Things That Happened Recently Are More Likely to Happen Again?" Decision Lab, https://thedecisionlab.com/biases/availability-heuristic.

Chapter Three: Loneliness

1 Joe Brownstein, "Want to Be Happy? Stop Trying," Live Science, May 19, 2011, https://www.livescience.com/14229-happiness-factors.html.

2 "New Cigna Study Reveals Loneliness at Epidemic Levels in
   America," Cigna.com, May 1, 2018, https://www.cigna.com/
   newsroom/news-releases/2018/new-cigna-study-reveals
   -loneliness-at-epidemic-levels-in-america.

3 Bianca DiJulio, Liz Hamel, Cailey Munana, and Mollyann Drodie,
   "Loneliness and Social Isolation in the United States, the United
   Kingdom, and Japan: An International Survey," Kaiser Family
   Foundation, August 30, 2018, https://www.kff.org/report-section/
   loneliness-and-social-isolation-in-the-united-states-the-united
   -kingdom-and-japan-an-international-survey-section-1/.

4 Larry J. Siegel and Chris McCormick, *Criminology in Canada:
   Theories, Patterns, and Typologies*, 3rd ed. (Toronto: Thompson
   Educational Publishing, 2006).

5 Julianne Holt-Lunstad, Timothy B. Smith, Mark Baker, Tyler
   Harris, and David Stephenson, "Loneliness and Social Isolation
   as Risk Factors for Mortality: A Meta-Analytic Review," BYU
   ScholarsArchive, March 23, 2015, https://scholarsarchive.byu
   .edu/cgi/viewcontent.cgi?article=3024&context=facpub.

6 Mental Health Information—Statistics—Suicide, National
   Institute of Mental Health, April 2019, https://www.nimh.nih
   .gov/health/statistics/suicide.shtml.

7 Francesca Friday, "More Americans Are Single Than Ever
   Before—and They're Healthier, Too," *Observer*, January 16, 2018,
   https://observer.com/2018/01/more-americans-are-single-than
   -ever-before-and-theyre-healthier-too/.

8 Chris Sherwood, Dr. Dylan Kneale, and Barbara Bloomfield, "The
   Way We Are Now," Relate, August 2014, https://www.relate.org.uk/
   sites/default/files/publication-way-we-are-now-aug2014_1.pdf.

9 Hakan Ozcelik and Sigal Barsade, "No Employee an Island:
   Workplace Loneliness and Job Performance," *Academy of
   Management Journal* 61, no. 6 (February 2018), https://www
   .researchgate.net/publication/323007916_No_employee_an
   _island_Workplace_loneliness_and_job_performance.

10 Sherwood, Kneale, and Bloomfield, "The Way We Are Now."

11 K. Reinking and R. Bell, "Relationships among Loneliness, Communication Competence, and Career Success in a State Bureaucracy: A Field Study of the 'Lonely at the Top' Maxim," *Communication Quarterly* 39, no. 4 (1991): 358–73, cited in Ami Rokach, ed., *Loneliness Updated: Recent Research on Loneliness and How It Affects Our Lives* (New York: Routledge, 2013), 51.

12 "1 in 3 Americans Can't Eat a Meal without Being on Their Phone," Nutrisystem Newsroom, January 23, 2018, https://newsroom.nutrisystem.com/1-in-3-americans-cant-eat-a-meal-without-being-on-their-phone/.

13 Jeffrey M. Jones, "U.S. Church Membership Down Sharply in Past Two Decades," Gallup, April 18, 2019, https://news.gallup.com/poll/248837/church-membership-down-sharply-past-two-decades.aspx.

14 Kristen Bialik, "Americans Unhappy with Family, Social or Financial Life Are More Likely to Say They Feel Lonely," Pew Research Center, December 3, 2018, https://www.pewresearch.org/fact-tank/2018/12/03/americans-unhappy-with-family-social-or-financial-life-are-more-likely-to-say-they-feel-lonely/.

15 Marc J. Dunkelman, *The Vanishing Neighbor: The Transformation of American Community* (New York: W. W. Norton & Company, 2014), xi–xii.

16 Robert Waldinger, MD, dir., "Harvard Study of Adult Development," https://www.adultdevelopmentstudy.org/.

Chapter Four: Negative Addictions

1 Tom Ferry with Laura Morton, *Life! By Design: 6 Steps to an Extraordinary You* (New York: Ballantine Books, 2010).

2 Jane, "6 Core Human Needs by Anthony Robbins," Habits for Wellbeing, nd, https://www.habitsforwellbeing.com/6-core-human-needs-by-anthony-robbins/.

3 "Drugs, Brains, and Behavior: The Science of Addiction," National Institute on Drug Abuse, July 2020, https://www.drugabuse.gov/publications/drugs-brains-behavior-science-addiction/drug-misuse-addiction.

4 Patrick Spröte and Rolan W. Fleming, "Concavities, Negative Parts, and the Perception That Shapes Are Complete," *Journal of Vision* 13, no. 14 (December 4, 2013): 3, https://pubmed.ncbi.nlm.nih.gov/24306852/.

Chapter Five: The Value of Connection

1 Maria Popova, "The Central Paradox of Love: Esther Perel on Reconciling the Closeness Needed for Intimacy with the Psychological Distance That Fuels Desire," Brain Pickings, https://www.brainpickings.org/2016/10/13/mating-in-captivity-esther-perel/.

2 "Sleep and Mental Health," Harvard Health Publishing, March 18, 2019, https://www.health.harvard.edu/newsletter_article/sleep-and-mental-health.

3 Daniel Kahneman, Alan B. Krueger, David A. Schkade, Norbert Schwarz, and Arthur A. Stone. "A Survey Method for Characterizing Daily Life Experience: The Day Reconstruction Method." *Science* 306, no. 5702 (December 3, 2004): 1776–80; https://www.ncbi.nlm.nih.gov/pubmed/15576620.

Chapter Six: Connecting with Others

1 Robert Weiss, PhD, "The Opposite of Addiction Is Connection," *Psychology Today*, September 30, 2015, https://www.psychologytoday.com/us/blog/love-and-sex-in-the-digital-age/201509/the-opposite-addiction-is-connection.

2 Kelly McGonigal, *The Upside of Stress: Why Stress Is Good for You, and How to Get Good at It*, Kindle edition (New York: Penguin, 2015).

3 Ray Oldenburg, *The Great Good Place*, Kindle edition (New York: Da Capo Press, 1989).

4 Kate Hood, "The Benefits of Active Constructive Responding,"
   Institute of Positive Education, https://www.ggs.vic.edu.au/Blog
   -Posts/the-benefits-of-active-constructive-responding.

Chapter Seven: A Bend in the Road
Is Not the End of the Road

1 David D. Burns, MD, Feeling Good (website), https://feelinggood
   .com/.

Chapter Eight: Positive Addictions

1 William Glasser, MD, *Positive Addiction* (New York: Harper
   Perennial, 1976).
2 Dr. Dan Gartrell, "Readiness: Not a State of Knowledge, but
   a State of Mind," National Association for the Education
   of Young Children, 2013, https://families.naeyc.org/
   learning-and-development/child-development/readiness-not
   -state-knowledge-state-mind.
3 Eric Berne, *Transactional Analysis in Psychotherapy* (Castle
   Books, 1961).

Chapter Nine: Motivation for a Happy Life

1 Mel Robbins, *The 5 Second Rule: Transform Your Life, Work, and
   Confidence with Everyday Courage*, Kindle edition (Nashville,
   TN: Savio Republic, 2017).
2 A. E. Ivey, N. B. Gluckstern, and M. B. Ivey, *Basic Influencing
   Skills*, 3rd ed. (Amherst, MA: Microtraining Associates, 1997),
   cited in William R. Miller, PhD, *Enhancing Motivation for
   Change in Substance Abuse Treatment* (Rockville, MD: Center
   for Substance Abuse Treatment, US Department of Health and
   Human Services, 1999).
3 Martin E. P. Seligman, PhD, *Authentic Happiness: Using the
   New Positive Psychology to Realize Your Potential for Lasting
   Fulfillment*, Kindle edition (New York: Free Press, 2002).

4 J. A. Tucker, R. E. Vuchinich, and J. A. Gladsjo, "Environmental
   Events Surrounding Natural Recovery from Alcohol-Related
   Problems," *Journal of Studies on Alcohol* 55, no. 4 (July 1994):
   401–11; and L. C. Sobell, M. B. Sobell, T. Toneatto, and G. I.
   Leo, "What Triggers the Resolution of Alcohol Problems without
   Treatment?" *Alcoholism, Clinical and Experimental Research*
   17, no. 2 (April 1993): 217–24; both cited in Miller, *Enhancing
   Motivation for Change.*

5 S. M. Varney, D. J. Rohsenow, A. N. Dey, M. G. Myers, W. R.
   Zwick, and P. M. Monti, "Factors Associated with Help Seeking
   and Perceived Dependence among Cocaine Users," *American
   Journal of Drug and Alcohol Abuse* 21, no. 1 (February 1995):
   81–91, cited in Miller, *Enhancing Motivation for Change.*

6 D. T. Gilbert and Timothy D. Wilson, "Miswanting: Some Problems
   in the Forecasting of Future Affective States" in *Thinking and
   Feeling: The Role of Affect in Social Cognition*, edited by Joseph P.
   Forgas (Cambridge: Cambridge University Press, 2000), 178–97,
   https://dash.harvard.edu/handle/1/14549983.

7 "How Does Misfortune Affect Long-Term Happiness?" *TED
   Radio Hour*, NPR, February 14, 2014, https://www.npr.org/
   transcripts/271144389.

8 Sonja Lyubomirsky, *The How of Happiness: A New Approach to
   Getting the Life You Want* (New York: Penguin, 2008); http://
   thehowofhappiness.com/.

9 Ibid.

Chapter Ten: Becoming an Ingenious Survivor during Dystopian Times

1 Flavia Medrut, "25 Johann Wolfgang von Goethe Quotes That
   Will Change the Way You See Yourself and Others," Goalcast,
   https://www.goalcast.com/2019/04/02/johann-wolfgang-von
   -goethe-quotes/.

2 Emily High, "Navigating Happiness amidst COVID-19; Key
   Outcomes from World Happiness Report Webinar," Sustainable

Development Solutions Network, March 23, 2020, https://
www.unsdsn.org/navigating-happiness-amidst-covid-19-key
-outcomes-from-world-happiness-report-webinar.

3 Daniel Gilbert, *Stumbling on Happiness* (New York: Alfred A. Knopf, 2006).

4 High, "Navigating Happiness amidst COVID-19."

5 Daniel J. Siegel, *The Developing Mind: How Relationships and the Brain Interact to Shape Who We Are* (New York: Guilford Press, 1999).

6 Dacher Keltner, "Why Do We Feel Awe?" Mindful, May 11, 2016, https://www.mindful.org/why-do-we-feel-awe/.

7 Emma Stone, PhD, "The Emerging Science of Awe and Its Benefits," *Psychology Today*, April 27, 2017, https://www.psychologytoday.com/us/blog/understanding-awe/201704/the-emerging-science-awe-and-its-benefits.

8 Keltner, "Why Do We Feel Awe?"

9 Elizabeth Dunn and Michael Norton, *Happy Money: The Science of Happier Spending* (New York: Simon & Schuster, 2013).

10 Martin E. P. Seligman, PhD, *Authentic Happiness: Using the New Positive Psychology to Realize Your Potential for Lasting Fulfillment*, Kindle edition (New York: Free Press, 2002).

11 Philippe Douyon, MD, *Neuroplasticity: Your Brain's Superpower* (Salt Lake City, UT: Izzard Ink, 2019).

12 Seligman, *Authentic Happiness*.

13 Mihaly Csikszentmihalyi, *Flow: The Psychology of Optimal Experience* (New York: Harper & Row, 1990).

14 Terrence Real, *The New Rules of Marriage: What You Need to Know to Make Love Work* (New York: Ballantine Books, 2007).

15 Viktor E. Frankl, *Man's Search for Meaning* (Vienna: Verlag für Jugend und Volk, 1946).

16 Jack Saul, *Collective Trauma, Collective Healing: Resilience in the Aftermath of Disaster* (New York: Routledge, 2014).

17 Gilbert, *Stumbling on Happiness*.

18 David Kessler, *Finding Meaning: The Sixth Stage of Grief* (New York: Scribner, 2019).

19 Sonja Lyubomirsky, *The How of Happiness: A Scientific Approach to Getting the Life You Want* (New York: Penguin, 2007).

20 John Gottman, PhD, *Why Marriages Succeed or Fail: And How You Can Make Yours Last* (New York: Simon & Schuster, 1994).

21 Christopher Kukk, "Survival of the Fittest Has Evolved; Try Survival of the Kindest," Better by *Today*, March 8, 2017, https://www.nbcnews.com/better/relationships/survival-fittest-has-evolved-try-survival-kindest-n730196.

about the author

Joan Neehall, PhD, is a clinical psychologist with a specialization in forensic psychology. She has practiced in Edmonton since 1984 (registration #1579) and in British Columbia from 1987 to 2019 (registration #922). She holds diplomate status in the American College of Forensic Examiners. Joan is a psychologist, author, wife, mother, and philanthropist, and conducted seminars in Shanghai, China, in 2019 and in Beijing in 2018. In addition to *Happy Is the New Healthy*, she has written *Perfecting Your Private Practice* (2004) and *Women Who Roar: Female Pioneers in Alberta* (2011), and she coauthored the bestselling *Habit of a Happy Life: 30 Days to a Positive Addiction* with Dr. Jeffrey Zeig, PhD, in 2018. She has appeared on television shows discussing a variety of topics ranging from body dysmorphia to stress management, as well as the new science of happiness. She taught at Simon Fraser University and has worked in hospitals and in private practice. In January 2020 she was invited to speak to dermatologists in Alberta on the topic of happiness. She participated in the Mindful Life Summit in San Francisco in February 2020.

Praise for *Happy Is the New Healthy*

"Eminent psychologist Dr. Joan Neehall provides witty, practical, and up-to-date information replete with engaging case studies. Have you missed some vibrant dance steps on your life path? *Happy Is the New Healthy* will help you reclaim joyful rhythms."

JEFFREY K. ZEIG, Ph.D., Director, The Milton H. Erickson Foundation

"If your attempts at discovering real happiness have left you feeling discouraged and disillusioned, take heart. This uncannily timely book provides a roadmap to help you avoid predictable dead ends and find lasting solutions for feeling more joy in your life."

MICHELE WEINER-DAVIS, Author of *Healing from Infidelity*,
Watch TEDx Talk "The Sex-Starved Marriage"

"Is there anything more important in life than health? But health never happens without happiness. . . . Dr. Joan Neehall, PhD, not only explores the ways to happiness of the mind but brings to life the concept of psychology of the immune system: a happy mind is a happy immune system."

DR. SVETA SILVERMAN, Associate Clinical Professor,
Department of Laboratory Medicine & Pathology

"[Dr. Neehall] describes that the pursuit of happiness frequently leads to unwanted states or negative addictions. Instead, she proposes that we develop positive addictions that support our happiness. She describes the basic building blocks of happiness such as connections to family, friends, and community; the physiological ingredients of happiness; and effective strategies to help us deal with the inevitable adversities of life."

KALOYAN TANEV, MD, Director of Clinical Neuropsychiatry Research,
Assistant Professor of Psychiatry at Massachusetts General Hospital

"*Happy Is the New Healthy* is an outstanding toolkit to help us understand the nature of happiness and how to work toward it. . . . Dr. Neehall provides us with an inspirational roadmap that is enjoyable, practical, rational, and ultimately motivating. This brilliantly written book is packed with highly engaging insights and logical instruction for all readers. With real-world examples and easy-to-follow directions, this guide should be mandatory reading for all *students of happiness* and *seekers of personal success*."

JAGGI RAO, MD, FRCPC, Clinical Professor of Medicine, University of Alberta